# Meeting SEN

## in the Curriculum:

## ENGLISH

## Other titles in the Meeting Special Needs in the Curriculum series:

# Meeting SEN in the Curriculum:

# ENGLISH

**Tim Hurst**

 **David Fulton** Publishers

David Fulton Publishers Ltd
The Chiswick Centre, 414 Chiswick High Road, London W4 5TF

www.fultonpublishers.co.uk

First published in Great Britain in 2004 by David Fulton Publishers

10   9   8   7   6   5   4   3   2   1

Note: the right of Tim Hurst to be identified as the author of this work has been asserted by him in accordance with the Copyright, Designs and Patents Act 1988.

Copyright © Tim Hurst 2004

*British Library Cataloguing in Publication Data*
A catalogue record for this book is available from the British Library.

David Fulton Publishers is a division of Granada Learning, part of ITV plc.

ISBN 1 84312 157 3

Typeset by Servis Filmsetting Ltd, Manchester
Printed and bound in Great Britain

# Contents

*To my wife Jane – whose support, encouragement and advice has been invaluable.*

# Contributors to the Series

## The author

**Tim Hurst** has been a SEN co-ordinator in five schools. His current post is at King Edward VI School, Bury St Edmunds, and he started his career at the Willian school in Hertfordshire as an English teacher. Tim later became second in the English department at that school and at about the same time became interested in what was then termed remedial English. Tim has always been committed to the idea of inclusion and the concept of a whole-school approach to special educational needs, particularly after studying for an Advanced Diploma in Special Educational Needs with the Open University. He is especially interested in the role and use of language in teaching.

A dedicated team of SEN specialists and subject specialists have contributed to the *Meeting Special Needs in the Curriculum* series.

## Series editor

**Alan Combes** started teaching in South Yorkshire in 1967 and was Head of English at several secondary schools before taking on the role of Head of PSHE as part of being senior teacher at Pindar School, Scarborough. He took early retirement to focus on his writing career and has authored two citizenship textbooks as well as writing several features for the TES. He has been used as an adviser on citizenship by the DfES and has emphasised citizenship's importance for special needs pupils as a speaker for NASEN.

## SEN specialists

**Sue Briggs** is a freelance education consultant based in Hereford. She writes and speaks on inclusion, special educational needs and disability, and Autistic Spectrum Disorders, and is a lay member of the SEN and Disability Tribunal. Until recently, she was SEN Inclusion Co-ordinator for Herefordshire Education Directorate. Originally trained as a secondary music teacher, Sue has extensive experience in mainstream and special schools. For six years she was teacher in charge of a language disorder unit.

**Sue Cunningham** is a learning support co-ordinator at a large mainstream secondary school in the West Midlands, where she manages a large team of learning support teachers and assistants. She has experience of working in both mainstream and special schools and has set up and managed a resource base for pupils with moderate learning difficulties in the mainstream as part of an initiative to promote a more inclusive education for pupils with SEN.

**Sally McKeown** is an Education Officer with Becta, the government funded agency responsible for managing the National Grid for Learning. She is responsible for the use of IT for learners with disabilities, learning difficulties or additional needs. She is a freelance journalist for the Times Educational Supplement and a regular contributor to disability magazines and to *Special Children* magazine. In 2001 her book *Unlocking Potential* was shortlisted for the NASEN Special Needs Book Award.

## Subject specialists

### Maths

**Brian Sharp** is a Key Stage 3 Mathematics consultant for Herefordshire. Brian has long experience of working both in special and mainstream schools as a teacher of mathematics. He has a range of management experience, including SENCO, mathematics and ICT co-ordinator.

### Science

**Carol Holden** works as a science teacher and assistant SENCO in a mainstream secondary school. She has developed courses for pupils with SEN within science and has gained a graduate diploma and MA in Educational Studies, focusing on SEN.

### Modern foreign languages

**Sally McKeown** is responsible for language-based work in the Inclusion team at Becta. She has a particular interest in learning difficulties and dyslexia. She writes regularly for the *TES*, *Guardian* and *Special Children* magazines.

### History

**Richard Harris** has been teaching since 1989. He has taught in three comprehensive schools, as history teacher, Head of Department and Head of Faculty. He has also worked as teacher consultant for secondary history in West Berkshire.

**Ian Luff** is assistant head teacher of Kesgrave High School, Suffolk and has been Head of history in three comprehensive schools.

### ICT

**Mike North** works for ICTC, an independent consultancy specialising in the effective use of ICT in education. He develops educational materials and provides advice and support for the SEN sector.

**Sally McKeown** is an Education Officer with Becta, the government funded agency responsible for managing the National Grid for Learning and the FERL website. She is responsible for the use of IT for learners with disabilities, learning difficulties or additional needs.

## Design and technology

**Louise T. Davies** is Principal Officer for Design and Technology at Qualifications and Curriculum Authority and also a freelance consultant. She is an experienced presenter and author of award-winning resources and books for schools. She chairs the Special Needs Advisory Group for the Design and Technology Association.

## Religious education

**Dilwyn Hunt** has worked as a specialist RE adviser, first in Birmingham and now in Dudley. He has a wide range of experience in the teaching of RE, including mainstream and special RE.

## Music

**Victoria Jaquiss** is SEN specialist for music with children with emotional and behavioural difficulties in Leeds. She devised a system of musical notation primarily for use with steel pans, for which, in 2002, she was awarded the fellowship of the Royal Society of Arts.

**Diane Paterson** works as an inclusive music curriculum teacher in Leeds.

## Geography

**Diane Swift** is a project leader for the Geographical Association. Her interest in special needs developed whilst she was a Staffordshire geography adviser and inspector.

## PE and sport

**Crispin Andrews** is an education/sports writer with nine years' experience of teaching and sports coaching.

## Art

**Kim Earle** is Able Pupils Consultant for St Helens and has been a Head of art and design. Kim is also a practising designer jeweller.

**Gill Curry** is Gifted and Talented Strand Co-ordinator for the Wirral. She has twenty years' experience as Head of art and has been an art advisory teacher. She is also a practising artist specialising in print.

# Contents of the CD

The CD contains activities and record sheets which can be amended/individualised and printed out for use by the purchasing institution.

Increasing the font size and spacing will improve accessibility for some students, as will changes in background colour. Alternatively, print onto pastel-coloured paper for greater ease of reading.

**Special Educational Needs Policy**
Fundamental Principes of the Special Needs Code of Practice
Definition of SEN (table)
App. 1.1
App. 1.2
App. 2.1
App. 2.2
Draft Spelling Policy

**Different Types of SEN**
Asperger's Syndrome
Attention Deficit Disorder (ADD)
Autistic Spectrum Disorders (ASD)
Behavioral, emotional and social difficulties
Cerebral Palsy
Down's Syndrome
Fragile X Syndrome
Moderate Learning Difficulties
Physical Disability
Semantic Pragmatic Disorder
Sensory Impairments
Visual Impairments
Severe Learning Difficulties
Profound and Multiple Learning Difficulties
Specific Learning Difficulties
Speech, Language and Communication Difficulties
Tourette's Syndrome

**The Inclusive Classroom**
The Students' point of view
Reading for Learning
Readability
Supporting Writers
The Four Stages of Writing

Using a spell-checker
Literacy Progress Units
Lesson Plan
Key Words and Spelling Policy

**Managing Support**
General guidelines for support
Subject teacher – support assistant agreement

**Case studies and IEPs**
Kuli (Hearing Impairment)
Harry (Dyslexia)
Megan (Wheelchair user)
Steven (EBSD)
Matthew (Cognitive Difficulties)
Bhavini (Visual Impairment)
Susan (Complex difficulties, ASD)
Jenny (Down's Syndrome)
IEPs from King Edward VI School

**Classroom resources**
Turntaking
Speaking frames
The Furbles of Tarp (Reading for meaning)
Who wants to be a millionaire? (Spelling and vocabulary practice)
Vocabulary building game
'The Assassin': plot, character and setting
Written response to *Macbeth*
How to paint a bathroom wall (writing instructions)
Fact and opinion
Writing frame for critical evaluation of a poem

Homework ideas
Pupil self-evaluation sheet

# Introduction

> All children have the right to a good education and the opportunity to fulfil their potential. All teachers should expect to teach children with special educational needs (SEN) and all schools should play their part in educating children from the local community, whatever their background or ability. (*Removing Barriers to Achievement: The Government's Strategy for SEN*, Feb 2004)

A raft of legislation and statutory guidance over the past few years has sought to make our mainstream education system more inclusive and ensure that pupils with a diverse range of ability and need are well catered for. This means that all staff need to have an awareness of how children learn and develop in different ways, and an understanding of how barriers to achievement can be removed – or at least minimised.

These barriers often result from inappropriate teaching styles, inaccessible teaching materials or ill-advised grouping of pupils, as much as from an individual child's physical, sensory or cognitive impairments: a fact which is becoming better understood. It is this developing understanding that is now shaping the legislative and advisory landscape of our education system, and making it necessary for all teachers to carefully reconsider their curriculum planning and classroom practice.

The major statutory requirements and non-statutory guidance are summarised in Chapter 1, setting the context for this resource and providing useful starting points for departmental INSET.

It is clear that provision for pupils with special educational needs (SEN) is not the sole responsibility of the SENCO and his or her team of assistants. If, in the past, subject teachers have 'taken a back seat' in the planning and delivery of a suitable curriculum for these children and expected the Learning Support department to bridge the gap between what was on offer in the classroom and what they actually needed, they can no longer do so. *The Code of Practice, 2002* states:

> All teaching and non teaching staff should be involved in the development of the school's SEN policy and be fully aware of the school's procedure for identifying, assessing and making provision for pupils with SEN.

Chapter 2 looks at departmental policy for SEN provision and provides useful audit material for reviewing and developing current practice.

The term 'special educational needs' is now widely used and has become something of a catch-all descriptor – rendering it less than useful in many cases. Before the Warnock Report (1978) and subsequent introduction of the term 'special educational needs', any pupils who for whatever reason – cognitive difficulties, emotional and behavioural difficulties, speech and language disorders – progressed more slowly than the 'norm' were designated 'remedials' and grouped together in the bottom sets, without the benefit, in many cases, of specialist subject teachers.

But the SEN tag was also applied to pupils in special schools who had more significant needs and had previously been identified as 'disabled' or even 'uneducable'. Add to these the deaf pupils, those with impaired vision, others with mobility problems, and even children from other countries with a limited understanding of the English language – who may or may not have been highly intelligent – and you have a recipe for confusion, to say the least.

The day-to-day descriptors used in the staffroom are gradually being moderated and refined as greater knowledge and awareness of special needs is built up. (We still hear staff describing pupils as 'totally thick', a 'nutcase' or 'complete moron' – but, hopefully, only as a means of letting off steam!) However, there are terms in common use which, though more measured and well-meaning, can still be unhelpful and misleading. Teachers will describe a child as being 'dyslexic' when they mean that he is poor at reading and writing; 'ADHD' has become a synonym for badly behaved; and a child who seems to be withdrawn or just eccentric is increasingly described as 'autistic'. (Of course, the use of 'he' includes both male and female pupils throughout the book.)

The whole process of applying labels is fraught with danger, but sharing a common vocabulary – and more importantly, a common understanding – can help colleagues to express their concerns about a pupil and address the issues as they appear in the classroom. Often, this is better achieved by identifying the particular areas of difficulty experienced by the pupil rather than by identifying the syndrome. The Code of Practice identifies four main areas of difficulty and these are detailed in Chapter 3 – along with an 'at a glance' guide to a wide range of syndromes and conditions, and guidance on how they might present barriers to learning.

There is no doubt that the number of children with special needs being educated in mainstream schools is growing:

> . . . because of the increased emphasis on the inclusion of children with SEN in mainstream schools the number of these children is increasing, as are the severity and variety of their SEN. Children with a far wider range of learning difficulties and variety of medical conditions, as well as sensory difficulties and physical disabilities, are now attending mainstream classes. The implication of this is that mainstream school teachers need to expand their knowledge and skills with regard to the needs of children with SEN. (Stakes and Hornby 2000:3)

The continuing move to greater inclusion means that all teachers can now expect to teach pupils with varied, and quite significant, special educational needs at some time. Even five years ago, it was rare to come across children with Asperger's/Down's/Tourette's Syndrome, Autistic Spectrum Disorder or significant physical/sensory disabilities in community secondary schools. Now, they are entering mainstream education in growing numbers, and there is a realisation that their 'inclusion' cannot be simply the responsibility of the SENCO and support staff. All staff have to be aware of particular learning needs and able to employ strategies in the classroom that directly address those needs.

Chapter 4 considers the components of an inclusive classroom and how the physical environment and resources, structure of the lesson and teaching approaches can make a real difference to pupils with special needs.

The monitoring of pupils' achievements and progress is a key factor in identifying and meeting their learning needs. Those pupils who make slower progress than their peers are often working just as hard, or even harder, but their efforts can go unrewarded. Chapter 5 addresses the importance of target setting and subsequent assessment and review in acknowledging pupils' achievements and in showing the department's effectiveness in value-added terms.

Liaising with the SENCO and support staff is an important part of every teacher's role. The SENCO's status in a secondary school often means that this teacher is part of the leadership team and influential in shaping whole-school policy and practice. Specific duties might include:

- ensuring liaison with parents and other professionals;

- advising and supporting teaching and support staff;

- ensuring that appropriate Individual Education Plans are in place;

- ensuring that relevant background information about individual children with special educational needs is collected, recorded and updated;

- making plans for future support and setting targets for improvement;

- monitoring and reviewing action taken.

The SENCO has invariably undergone training in different aspects of special needs provision and has much to offer colleagues in terms of in-house training and advice about appropriate materials to use with pupils. The SENCO should be a frequent and valuable point of reference for all staff, but is often overlooked in this capacity. The presence of the SENCO at the occasional departmental meeting can be very effective in developing teachers' skills in relation to meeting SEN, making them aware of new initiatives and methodology and sharing information about individual children.

In most schools, however, the SENCO's skills and knowledge are channelled to the chalkface via a team of Teaching or Learning Support Assistants (TAs, LSAs). These assistants can be very able and well-qualified, but very underused in the classroom. Chapter 6 looks at how teachers can manage in-class support in a way that makes the best use of a valuable resource.

The revised regulations for SEN provision make it clear that mainstream schools are expected to provide for pupils with a wide diversity of needs, and teaching is evaluated on the extent to which all pupils are engaged and enabled to achieve.

This book has been produced in response to the implications of all of this for secondary subject teachers. It has been written by an English specialist with support from colleagues who have expertise within the SEN field, so that the information and guidance given is both subject specific and pedagogically sound. The book and accompanying CD provide a resource that can be used with colleagues:

- to shape departmental policy and practice for special needs provision;

- to enable staff to react with a measured response when inclusion issues arise;

- to ensure that every pupil achieves appropriately in English.

# Meeting Special Educational Needs – Your Responsibility

Inclusion in education involves the process of increasing the participation of students in, and reducing their exclusion from, the cultures, curricula and communities of local schools. (*The Index for Inclusion*, 2000)

*The Index for Inclusion* was distributed to all maintained schools by the Department for Education and Skills and has been a valuable tool for many schools as they have worked to develop their inclusive practice. It supports schools in the review of their policies, practices and procedures, and the development of an inclusive approach, and where it has been used as part of the school improvement process – looking at inclusion in the widest sense – it has been a great success. For many people, however, *The Index* lacked any real teeth and recent legislation and non-statutory guidance is more authoritative.

## The SEN and Disability Act 2001

The SEN and Disability Act 2001 Act amended the Disability Discrimination Act and created important new duties for schools. Under this Act, schools are obliged:

- to take reasonable steps to ensure that disabled pupils are not placed at a substantial disadvantage in relation to the education and other services they provide. This means they must anticipate where barriers to learning lie and take action to remove them as far as they are able;

- to plan strategically to increase the extent to which disabled pupils can participate in the curriculum, make the physical environment more accessible and ensure that written material is provided in accessible formats.

The reasonable steps taken might include:

- changing policies and practices;
- changing course requirements;

- changing the physical features of a building;

- providing interpreters or other support workers;

- providing alternative means of recording work such as using ICT, dictation machines;

- delivering courses in alternative ways – reducing the reading and writing load wherever possible without reducing the sense of challenge;

- providing materials in other formats.

It is good practice, for example, for a department to produce all materials in electronic form to ensure that they can easily be converted into large print or put into other alternative formats, such as Braille. The staff are then anticipating 'reasonable adjustments' that might need to be made.

See Appendix 1.1 and 1.2 for further detail on SENDA and INSET activities.

## The Revised National Curriculum

The Revised National Curriculum (2002) emphasises the provision of effective learning opportunities for all learners, and establishes three principles for promoting inclusion:

- setting suitable learning challenges

- responding to pupils' diverse learning needs

- overcoming potential barriers to learning and assessment

The National Curriculum guidance suggests that staff may need to differentiate tasks and materials, and facilitate access to learning by:

- encouraging pupils to use all available senses and experiences;

- planning for participation in all activities;

- helping children to manage their behaviour, take part in learning and prepare for work;

- helping pupils to manage their emotions;

- giving teachers, where necessary, the discretion to teach pupils material from earlier key stages, providing consideration is given to age-appropriate learning contexts. (This means that a fourteen-year-old with significant learning difficulties may be taught relevant aspects of the Programmes of Study (PoS) for English at Key Stage 3, but at the same time might be working on suitable material founded in the PoS for Key Stage 1.)

The Qualifications and Curriculum Authority (QCA) have also introduced performance descriptions (P levels/P scales) to enable teachers to observe and record small steps of progress made by some pupils with SEN. These descriptions outline early learning and attainment for each subject in the National Curriculum, including citizenship, RE and PSHE. They chart progress up to NC level 1 through eight steps. The performance descriptions for P1 to P3 are common across all subjects and outline the types and range of general performance that some pupils with learning difficulties might characteristically demonstrate. From level P4 onwards, many believe it is possible to describe performance in a way that indicates the emergence of subject-focused skills, knowledge and understanding.

## The Code of Practice for special educational needs

The Revised Code of Practice (implemented in 2002) describes a cyclical process of planning, target-setting and review for pupils with SEN. It also makes clear the expectation that the vast majority of pupils with special needs will be educated in mainstream settings. Those identified as needing over and above what the school can provide from its own resources, however, are nominated for 'School Action Plus' and outside agencies will be involved in planned intervention. This may involve professionals from the Learning Support Service, a specialist teacher or therapist, or an educational psychologist, working with the school's SENCO to put together an Individual Education Plan (IEP) for the pupil. In a minority of cases (the numbers vary widely between LEAs), pupils may be assessed by a multi-disciplinary team on behalf of the local education authority, whose representatives then decide whether or not to issue a statement of SEN. This is a legally binding document detailing the child's needs and setting out the resources which should be provided. It is reviewed every year.

> Fundamental Principles of the Special Needs Code of Practice:
> - A child with special educational needs should have their needs met.
> - The special educational needs of children will normally be met in mainstream schools or settings.
> - The views of the child should be sought and taken into account.
> - Parents have a vital role to play in supporting their child's education.
> - Children with special educational needs should be offered full access to a broad, balanced and relevant education, including an appropriate curriculum for the Foundation stage and the National Curriculum.

## Ofsted

Ofsted inspectors are required to make judgements about a school's inclusion policy, and how this is translated into practice in individual classrooms. According to Ofsted (2003), the following key factors help schools to become more inclusive:

- a climate of acceptance of all pupils

- careful preparation of placements for SEN pupils within teaching groups – taking account of social factors *(for example, whatever pedagogic justification we may make for creating 'bottom sets', it may not prevent teachers from having low expectations and students from developing poor self-image)*

- availability of sufficient suitable teaching and personal support

- widespread awareness among staff of the particular needs of SEN pupils and an understanding of the practical ways of meeting these needs in the classroom

- sensitive allocation to teaching groups and careful curriculum modification, timetables and social arrangements

- availability of appropriate materials and teaching aids and adapted accommodation

- an active approach to personal and social development, as well as to learning

- well-defined and consistently applied approaches to managing difficult behaviour

- assessment, recording and reporting procedures which can embrace and express adequately the progress of pupils with more complex SEN who make only small gains in learning and PSD

- involving parents/carers as fully as possible in decision-making, keeping them well-informed about their child's progress and giving them as much practical support as possible

- developing and taking advantage of training opportunities, including links with special schools and other schools.

## Policy into practice

Effective teaching for pupils with SEN is, by and large, effective for all pupils, but as schools become more inclusive, teachers need to be able to respond to a wider range of needs. The Government's strategy for SEN (*Removing Barriers to Learning*, 2004) sets out ambitious proposals to 'help teachers expand their repertoire of inclusive skills and strategies and plan confidently to include children with increasingly complex needs'.

In many cases, pupils' individual needs will be met through greater differentiation of tasks and materials, i.e. school-based intervention as set out in the SEN Code of Practice. A smaller number of pupils may need access to specialist equipment and approaches or to alternative or adapted activities, as part of a 'School Action Plus' programme, augmented by advice and support from external specialists. The QCA, on its website 2003, encourages teachers to take specific action to provide access to learning for pupils with special educational needs by:

(a) providing for pupils who need help with communication, language and literacy through:

- using texts that pupils can read and understand. Staff need to have a clear understanding of readability issues and be able to implement appropriate strategies easily

- using visual and written materials in different formats, including large print, symbol text and Braille

- using ICT, other technological aids and taped materials

- using alternative and augmentative communication, including signs and symbols

- using translators, communicators and amanuenses

(b) planning, where necessary, to develop pupils' understanding through the use of all available senses and experiences by:

- using materials and resources that pupils can access through sight, touch, sound, taste or smell

- using word descriptions and other stimuli to make up for a lack of first-hand experiences

- using ICT, visual and other materials to increase pupils' knowledge of the wider world

- encouraging pupils to take part in everyday activities such as play, drama, class visits and exploring the environment

(c) planning for pupils' full participation in learning and in physical and practical activities by:

- using specialist aids and equipment

- providing support from adults or peers when needed

- adapting tasks or environments

- providing alternative activities, where necessary

(d) helping pupils to manage their behaviour, to take part in learning effectively and safely, and, at Key Stage 4, to prepare for work by:

- setting realistic demands and stating them explicitly

- using positive behaviour management, including a clear structure of rewards and sanctions

- giving pupils every chance and encouragement to develop the skills they need to work well with a partner or a group

- teaching pupils to value and respect the contribution of others

- encouraging and teaching independent working skills

- teaching essential safety rules

(e) helping individuals to manage their emotions, particularly trauma or stress, and to take part in learning by:

- identifying aspects of learning in which the pupil will engage and plan short-term, easily achievable goals in selected activities

- providing positive feedback to reinforce and encourage learning and build self-esteem

- selecting tasks and materials sensitively to avoid unnecessary stress for the pupil

- creating a supportive learning environment in which the pupil feels safe and is able to engage with learning

- allowing time for the pupil to engage with learning and gradually increasing the range of activities and demands.

## Pupils with disabilities

The QCA goes on to provide guidance on pupils with disabilities, pointing out that not all pupils with disabilities will necessarily have special educational needs. Many learn alongside their peers with little need for additional resources beyond the aids which they use as part of their daily life, such as a wheelchair, a hearing aid or equipment to aid vision. Teachers' planning must ensure, however, that these pupils are enabled to participate as fully and effectively as possible in the curriculum by:

(a) planning appropriate amounts of time to allow for the satisfactory completion of tasks. This might involve:

- taking account of the very slow pace at which some pupils will be able to record work, either manually or with specialist equipment, and of the physical effort required

- being aware of the high levels of concentration necessary for some pupils when following or interpreting text or graphics, particularly when using vision aids or tactile methods, and of the tiredness which may result

- allocating sufficient time, opportunity and access to equipment for pupils to gain information through experimental work and detailed observation, including the use of microscopes

- being aware of the effort required by some pupils to follow oral work, whether through use of residual hearing, lip reading or a signer, and of the tiredness or loss of concentration which may occur.

(b) planning opportunities, where necessary, for the development of skills in practical aspects of the curriculum. This might involve:

- providing adapted, modified or alternative activities or approaches to learning in English and ensuring that these have integrity and equivalence to the National Curriculum and enable pupils to make appropriate progress

- ensuring that all pupils can be included and participate safely in local visits to theatres and other sites.

(c) identifying aspects of Programmes of Study and attainment targets that may present specific difficulties for individuals.

*It is important for English teachers to remember that, while there is still more flexibility in English than in most subjects for the subject matter to be tailored more closely to the interests of the group, it can still represent for many students an encapsulation of everything that they hate, namely reading, writing and speaking.*

## Summary

Pupils with a wide range of needs – physical/sensory, emotional, cognitive and social – are present in increasing numbers, in all mainstream settings. Government policies point the way, with inclusion at the forefront of national policy – but it is up to teachers to make the rhetoric a reality. Teachers are ultimately responsible for all the children they teach. In terms of participation, achievement, enjoyment – the buck stops here!

# CHAPTER 2

# Departmental Policy

It is crucial that departmental policy describes a strategy for meeting pupils' special educational needs within the particular curricular area. The policy should set the scene for any visitor to the English department – from supply staff to inspectors – and make a valuable contribution to the departmental handbook. The process of developing a department SEN policy offers the opportunity to clarify and evaluate current thinking and practice within the English team and to establish a consistent approach.

The policy should:

- clarify the responsibilities of all staff and identify any with specialist training and/or knowledge;

- describe the curriculum on offer and how it can be differentiated;

- outline arrangements for assessment and reporting;

- guide staff on how to work effectively with support staff;

- identify staff training.

The starting point will be the school's SEN policy as required by the Education Act 1996, with each subject department 'fleshing out' the detail in a way which describes how things work in practice. The writing of a policy should be much more than a paper exercise completed to satisfy the senior management team and Ofsted inspectors: it is an opportunity for staff to come together as a team and create a framework for teaching English in a way that makes it accessible to all pupils in the school.

## Where to start when writing a policy

An audit can act as a starting point for reviewing current policy on SEN or it can inform the writing of a new policy. It will involve gathering information and reviewing current practice with regard to pupils with SEN, and is best completed by the whole of the department, preferably with some additional advice from the SENCO or another member of staff with responsibility for SEN within the school. An audit carried out by the whole department can provide a valuable opportunity for professional development if it is seen as an exercise in sharing good practice and encouraging joint planning. If your SEN department is engaged in a provision mapping exercise, this is even more reason to become involved. But before embarking on an audit, it is worth investing some time in a department meeting or training day, to raise awareness of special educational needs legislation and to establish a shared philosophy. Appendix 2.1 contains OHT layouts and an activity to use with staff. (These are also on the accompanying CD, with additional exercises you may choose to use.)

The following headings may be useful in establishing a working policy:

## General statement

- What does legislation and DfES guidance say?

- What does the school policy state?

- What do members of the department have to do to comply with it?

## Definition of SEN

- What does SEN mean?

- What are the areas of need and the categories used in the Code of Practice?

- Are there any special implications within the subject area?

## Provision for staff within the department

- How is information shared?

- Who has responsibility for SEN within the department?

- How and when is information shared?

- Where and what information is stored?

## Provision for pupils with SEN

- How are pupils with SEN assessed and monitored in the department?

- How are contributions to IEPs and reviews made?

- What criteria are used for organising teaching groups?

- What alternative courses are offered to pupils with SEN?

- What special internal and external examination arrangements are made?

- What guidance is available for working with support staff?

## Resources and learning materials

- Is there any specialist equipment used in the department?

- How are resources developed? What criteria do we use? What notice have we taken of given measure of ability in reading and writing and speaking?

- Where are resources stored?

## Staff qualifications and Continuing Professional Development needs

- What qualifications do the members of the department have? (One English department who carried out this sort of exercise found that they had an EAL expert and an ex-SEN Teaching Assistant in their midst.)

- What training has taken place?

- How is training planned?

- What account is taken of SEN when new training opportunities are proposed?

- Is a record kept of training completed and training needs?

## Monitoring and reviewing the policy

- How will the policy be monitored?

- When will the policy be reviewed?

## The content of a SEN departmental policy

This section gives detailed information on what a SEN policy might include. Each heading is expanded with some detailed information and raises the main issues with regard to teaching pupils with SEN. At the end of each section there is an example statement. The example statements can be personalised and brought together to make a policy. All the examples in this chapter are gathered as an example policy in Appendix 3.

## General statement with reference to the school's SEN policy

All schools must have a SEN policy according to the Education Act 1996. This policy will set out basic information on the school's SEN provision, how the school identifies, assesses and provides for pupils with SEN, including information on staffing and working in partnership with other professionals and parents.

Any department policy needs to have reference to the school SEN policy.

## Example

> All members of the department will ensure that the needs of all pupils with SEN are met, according to the aims of the school and its SEN policy.

## Definition of SEN

It is useful to insert at least the four areas of SEN in the department policy, as used in the Code of Practice for Special Educational Needs.

### TABLE 2.1 THE FOUR AREAS OF SEN

| Cognition and Learning Needs | Behavioural, Emotional and Social Development Needs | Communication and Interaction Needs | Sensory and/or Physical Needs |
|---|---|---|---|
| Specific learning difficulties (SpLD) | Behavioural, emotional and social difficulties (BESD) | Speech, language and communication needs | Hearing impairment (HI) |
| Moderate learning difficulties (MLD) | | Autistic Spectrum Disorders (ASD) | Visual impairment (VI) |
| Severe learning difficulties (SLD) | Attention Deficit Disorder (ADD) | Asperger's Syndrome | Multi-sensory impairment (MSI) |
| Profound and multiple learning difficulties (PMLD) | Attention Deficit Hyperactivity Disorder (ADHD) | | Physical difficulties (PD) |
| | | | OTHER |

## Provision for staff within the department

In many schools, each department nominates a member of staff to have special responsibility for SEN provision (with or without remuneration). This can be very effective where there is a system of regular liaison between department SEN representatives and the SENCO in the form of meetings or paper communications or a mixture of both.

The responsibilities of this post may include liaison between the department and the SENCO, attending any liaison meetings and providing feedback via meetings and minutes, attending training, maintaining the departmental SEN information and records and representing the needs of pupils with SEN at departmental level. This post can be seen as a valuable development opportunity for staff. The name of this person should be included in the policy.

How members of the department raise concerns about pupils with SEN can be included in this section. Concerns may be raised at specified departmental meetings before referral to the SENCO. An identified member of the department could make referrals to the SENCO and keep a record of this information.

Reference to working with support staff will include a commitment to planning and communication between staff. There may be information on inviting support staff to meetings, resources and lesson plans.

A reference to the centrally held lists of pupils with SEN and other relevant information will also be included in this section. A note about confidentiality of information should be included.

## Example

> The member of staff with responsibility for overseeing the provision of SEN within the department will attend liaison meetings and feedback to other members of the department. He will maintain the department's SEN information file, attend appropriate training and disseminate this to all departmental staff. All information will be treated with confidentiality.

## Provision for pupils with SEN

It is the responsibility of all staff to know which pupils have SEN and to identify any pupils having difficulties. Pupils with SEN may be identified by staff within the department in a variety of ways; these may be listed and could include:

- observation in lessons
- assessment of class work
- homework tasks
- end of module tests
- progress checks
- annual examinations
- reports

Setting out how pupils with SEN are grouped within the English department may include specifying the criteria used and/or the philosophy behind the method of grouping.

## Example

> The pupils are grouped according to ability as informed by Key Stage 2 results, reading scores and any other relevant performance, social or medical information.

We need to be careful in English that we are not bound solely by objective measures in reading and writing, but that we also take into account reasoning and oral abilities when we group students. It is also vital that personality issues are taken into account. Having a complement of good oral ability will lift the attitude and attainment of everybody within a group.

Monitoring arrangements and details of how pupils can move between groups should also be set out. Information collected may include:

- National Curriculum levels

- departmental assessments (being clear about the precise evidence they are based on)

- reading scores

- advice from pastoral staff

- discussion with staff in the SEN department

- information provided on IEPs

Special Examination arrangements need to be considered not only at Key Stage 3 and 4 but also for internal examinations. How and when these will be discussed should be clarified. Reference to SENCO and examination arrangements from the examination board should be taken into account. Ensuring that staff in the department understand the current legislation and guidance from central government is important, so a reference to the SEN Code of Practice and the levels of SEN intervention is helpful within the policy. Here is a good place also to put a statement about the school behaviour policy and rewards and sanctions, and how the department will make any necessary adjustments to meet the needs of pupils with SEN.

We need to remember that praise and reward cannot be overdone in any subject, but perhaps it particularly applies in English, with its emphasis on reading and writing – the two main areas with which children with SEN have traditionally struggled.

## Example

It is understood that pupils with SEN may receive additional support if they have a statement of SEN, are at School Action Plus or School Action. The staff in the English department will aim to support the pupils to achieve their targets as specified on their IEPs and will provide feedback for IEP or statement reviews. Pupils with SEN will be included in the departmental monitoring system used for all pupils. Additional support will be requested as appropriate.

## Resources and learning materials

The department policy needs to specify what differentiated materials are available, where they are kept and how to find new resources. This section could include a statement about working with support staff to develop resources or access specialist resources as needed, and the use of ICT. Teaching strategies may also be identified if appropriate. Advice on more specialist equipment can be sought as necessary, possibly through LEA support services: contact details may be available from the SENCO, or the department may have direct links. Any specially bought subject text or alternative/appropriate courses can be specified as well as any external assessment and examination courses.

### Example

The department will provide suitably differentiated materials, and where appropriate, specialist resources for pupils with SEN. Additional texts are available for those pupils working below National Curriculum level 3. At Key Stage 4 an alternative course to GCSE is offered at Entry level but, where possible, pupils with SEN will be encouraged to reach their full potential and follow a GCSE course. Support staff will be provided with curriculum information in advance of lessons and will also be involved in lesson planning. A list of resources is available in the department handbook and on the noticeboard.

## Staff qualifications and Continuing Professional Development needs

It is important to recognise and record the qualifications and special skills gained by staff within the department. Training can include not only external courses but also in-house INSET and opportunities such as observing other staff, working to produce materials with other staff, and visiting other establishments. Staff may have undisclosed skills that might enhance the work of the department and the school, for example, some staff might be proficient in the use of sign language. An audit of the varieties of expertise within a department may reveal teachers who are reckoned to have particular talents with regard to SEN students. If this is the case, it merits full investigation! Just what is it that they do which makes for such success? Observation of these teachers can be very beneficial.

### Example

A record of training undertaken, specialist skills and training required will be kept in the department handbook. Requests for training will be considered in line with the department and school improvement plan.

## Monitoring and reviewing the policy

Any policy to be effective needs regular monitoring and review. These can be planned as part of the yearly cycle. The responsibility for the monitoring can rest with the Head of Department, but will have more effect if supported by someone from another department outside acting as a critical friend. This could be the SENCO or a member of the senior management team in the school.

### Example

> The department SEN policy will be monitored by the Head of Department on a planned annual basis, with advice being sought from the SENCO as part of a three-yearly review process.

## Conclusion

Creating a departmental SEN policy should be a developmental activity to improve the teaching and learning for all pupils, but especially for those with special or additional needs. The policy should be a working document that will evolve and change; it is there to challenge current practice and to encourage improvement for both pupils and staff. If departmental staff work together to create the policy, they will have ownership of it; it will have true meaning and be effective in clarifying practice.

# Different Types of SEN

This chapter is a starting point for information on the special educational needs most frequently occurring in the mainstream secondary school. It describes the main characteristics of each learning difficulty, with practical ideas for use in subject areas and contacts for further information. Some of the tips are based on good secondary practice while others encourage teachers to try new or less familiar approaches.

The special educational needs outlined in this chapter are grouped under the headings used in the SEN Code of Practice (DfES 2001):

- cognition and learning

- behavioural, emotional and social development

- communication and interaction

- sensory and/or physical needs.

(See Table 2.1 in Chapter 2.)

The labels used in this chapter are useful when describing pupils' difficulties, but it is important to remember not to use the label in order to define the pupil. Put the pupil before the difficulty, saying 'the pupil with special educational needs' rather than 'the SEN pupil', 'pupils with MLD' rather than 'MLDs'. Students with Autistic Spectrum Disorder will present with vastly different personalities, just like anyone else.

Remember to take care in using labels when talking with parents, pupils or other professionals. Unless a pupil has a firm diagnosis, and parents and pupil understand the implications of that diagnosis, it is more appropriate to describe the features of the special educational need rather than use the label; for example, a teacher might describe a pupil's spelling difficulties but not use the term 'dyslexic'.

The number and profile of pupils with special educational needs will vary from school to school, so it is important to consider the pupil with SEN as an individual within your school and subject environment. The strategies contained in this chapter will help teachers adapt that environment to meet the needs of individual pupils within the subject context. For example, rather than saying, 'He can't read the worksheet', recognise that the worksheet is too difficult for the pupil, and adapt the work accordingly.

There is a continuum of need within each of the special educational needs listed here. Some pupils will be affected more than others, and show fewer or more of the characteristics described.

The availability and levels of support from professionals within a school (e.g. SENCOs, support teachers, Teaching Assistants) and external professionals (e.g. educational psychologists, Learning Support Service staff, medical staff) will depend on the severity of pupils' SEN. This continuum of need will also impact on the subject teacher's planning and allocation of support staff.

Pupils with other less common special educational needs may be included in some secondary schools, and additional information on these conditions may be found in a variety of sources. These include the school SENCO, LEA support services, educational psychologists and the Internet.

In Appendix 3 you will find case studies of eight pupils with a variety of special educational needs and suggested strategies for their English teachers.

## Asperger's Syndrome

Asperger's Syndrome is a disorder at the able end of the autistic spectrum. People with Asperger's Syndrome have average to high intelligence but share the same Triad of Impairments. They often want to make friends but do not understand the complex rules of social interaction. They have impaired fine and gross motor skills, with writing being a particular problem. Boys are more likely to be affected – with the ratio being 10:1 boys to girls. Because they appear 'odd' and naïve, these pupils are particularly vulnerable to bullying.

### Main characteristics:

- Social interaction
  Pupils with Asperger's Syndrome want friends but have not developed the strategies necessary for making and sustaining friendships. They find it very difficult to learn social norms and to pick up on social cues. Highly social situations, such as lessons, can cause great anxiety.

- Social communication
  Pupils have appropriate spoken language but tend to sound formal and pedantic, using little expression and with an unusual tone of voice. They have difficulty using and understanding non-verbal language such as facial expression, gesture, body language and eye-contact. They have a literal understanding of language and do not grasp implied meanings.

- Social imagination
  Pupils with Asperger's Syndrome need structured environments, and to have routines they understand and can anticipate. They excel at learning facts and figures, but have difficulty understanding abstract concepts and in generalising information and skills. They often have all-consuming special interests.

### How can the subject teacher help?

- Liaise closely with parents, especially over homework.
- Create as calm a classroom environment as possible.
- Allow to sit in the same place for each lesson.
- Set up a work buddy system for your lessons.
- Provide additional visual cues in class.
- Give time to process questions and respond.
- Make sure pupils understand what to do.
- Allow alternatives to writing for recording.
- Use visual timetables and task activity lists.
- Prepare for changes to routines well in advance.
- Give written homework instructions and stick into an exercise book.
- Have your own class rules and apply them consistently.

The National Autistic Society, 393 City Road, London ECIV 1NG
Tel: 0845 070 4004  Helpline (10am–4pm, Mon–Fri)  Tel: 020 7833 2299
Fax: 020 7833 9666
Email: nas@nas.org.uk  Website: http://www.nas.org.uk

# Attention Deficit Disorder (with or without hyperactivity) (ADD/ADHD)

Attention Deficit Hyperactivity Disorder is a term used to describe children who exhibit over-active behaviour and impulsivity and who have difficulty in paying attention. It is caused by a form of brain dysfunction of a genetic nature. ADHD can sometimes be controlled effectively by medication. Children of all levels of ability can have ADHD.

## Main characteristics.

- difficulty in following instructions and completing tasks
- easily distracted by noise, movement of others, objects attracting attention
- often doesn't listen when spoken to
- fidgets and becomes restless, can't sit still
- interferes with other pupils' work
- can't stop talking, interrupts others, calls out
- runs about when inappropriate
- has difficulty in waiting or taking turns
- acts impulsively without thinking about the consequences

## How can the subject teacher help?

- Make eye contact and use the pupil's name when speaking to him.
- Keep instructions simple – the one sentence rule.
- Provide clear routines and rules, and rehearse them regularly.
- Sit the pupil away from obvious distractions, e.g. windows, the computer.
- In busy situations direct the pupil by name to visual or practical objects.
- Encourage the pupil to repeat back instructions before starting work.
- Tell the pupil when to begin a task.
- Give two choices – avoid the option of the pupil saying 'no', e.g. 'Do you want to write in blue or black pen?'
- Give advanced warning when something is about to happen. Change or finish with a time, e.g. 'In two minutes I need you [pupil name] to . . . '
- Give specific praise – catch him being good, give attention for positive behaviour.
- Give the pupil responsibilities so that others can see him in a positive light and hr develops a positive self-image.

ADD Information Services, PO Box 340, Edgware, Middlesex HA8 9HL
Tel: 020 8906 9068
ADDNET UK Website: www.btinternet.com/~black.ice/addnet/

## Autistic Spectrum Disorders (ASD)

The term 'Autistic Spectrum Disorders' is used for a range of disorders affecting the development of social interaction, social communication, and social imagination and flexibility of thought. This is known as the 'Triad of Impairments'. Pupils with ASD cover the full range of ability, and the severity of the impairment varies widely. Some pupils also have learning disabilities or other difficulties. Four times as many boys as girls are diagnosed with an ASD.

### Main characteristics:

● Social interaction
Pupils with an ASD find it difficult to understand social behaviour and this affects their ability to interact with children and adults. They do not always understand social contexts. They may experience high levels of stress and anxiety in settings that do not meet their needs or when routines are changed. This can lead to inappropriate behaviour.

● Social communication
Understanding and use of non-verbal and verbal communication is impaired. Pupils with an ASD have difficulty understanding the communication of others and in developing effective communication themselves. They have a literal understanding of language. Many are delayed in learning to speak, and some never develop speech at all.

● Social imagination and flexibility of thought
Pupils with an ASD have difficulty in thinking and behaving flexibly, which may result in restricted, obsessional or repetitive activities. They are often more interested in objects than people, and have intense interests in one particular area, such as trains or vacuum cleaners. Pupils work best when they have a routine. Unexpected changes in those routines will cause distress. Some pupils with Autistic Spectrum Disorders have a different perception of sounds, sights, smell, touch, and taste, and this can affect their response to these sensations.

### How can the subject teacher help?

● Liaise with parents as they will have many useful strategies.
● Provide visual supports in class: objects, pictures, etc.
● Give a symbolic or written timetable for each day.
● Give advance warning of any changes to usual routines.
● Provide either an individual desk or with a work buddy.
● Avoid using too much eye contact as it can cause distress.
● Give individual instructions, using the pupil's name, e.g. 'Paul, bring me your book.'
● Allow access to computers.
● Develop social interactions using a buddy system or Circle of Friends.
● Avoid using metaphor, idiom or sarcasm – say what you mean in simple language.
● Use special interests to motivate.
● Allow difficult situations to be rehearsed by means of Social Stories.

## BEHAVIOURAL, EMOTIONAL AND SOCIAL DEVELOPMENT NEEDS

This term includes behavioural, emotional, social difficulties and Attention Deficit Disorder with or without hyperactivity. These difficulties can be seen across the whole ability range and have a continuum of severity. Pupils with special educational needs in this category are those who have persistent difficulties despite an effective school behaviour policy and a personal and social curriculum.

# Behavioural, emotional and social difficulties (BESD)

## Main characteristics:

- inattentive, poor concentration and lack of interest in school/school work
- easily frustrated, anxious about changes
- unable to work in groups
- unable to work independently, constantly seeking help
- confrontational – verbally aggressive towards pupils and/or adults
- physically aggressive towards pupils and/or adults
- destroys property – their own/others
- appears withdrawn, distressed, unhappy, sulky, may self-harm
- lacks confidence, acts extremely frightened, lacks self-esteem
- finds it difficult to communicate
- finds it difficult to accept praise

## How can the subject teacher help?

- Check the ability level of the pupil and adapt the level of work to this.
- Consider the pupil's strengths and use them.
- Tell the pupil what you expect in advance, as regards work and behaviour.
- Talk to the pupil to find out a bit about them.
- Set a subject target with a reward system.
- Focus your comments on the behaviour, not on the pupil, and offer an alternative way of behaving when correcting the pupil.
- Use positive language and verbal praise whenever possible.
- Tell the pupil what you want them to do – 'I need you to . . . , I want you to . . .' – rather than ask. This avoids confrontation and allows the possibility that there is room for negotiation.
- Give the pupil a choice between two options.
- Stick to what you say.
- Involve the pupil in responsibilities to increase self-esteem and confidence.
- Plan a 'time out' system. Ask a colleague for help with this.

SEBDA is the new name for the Association of Workers for Children with emotional and behavioural difficulties.
Website: www.awcelod.co.uk

## Cerebral palsy

Cerebral palsy is a persistent disorder of movement and posture. It is caused by damage or lack of development to part of the brain before or during birth or in early childhood. Problems vary from slight clumsiness to more severe lack of control of movements. Pupils with CP may also have learning difficulties. They may use a wheelchair or other mobility aid.

### Main characteristics:

There are three main forms of cerebral palsy:

- *spasticity* – disordered control of movement associated with stiffened muscles
- *athetosis* – frequent involuntary movements
- *ataxia* – an unsteady gait with balance difficulties and poor spatial awareness

  Pupils may also have communication difficulties.

### How can the subject teacher help?

- Talk to parents, the physiotherapist – and the pupil.
- Consider the classroom layout.
- Have high academic expectations.
- Use visual supports: objects, pictures, symbols.
- Arrange a work/subject buddy.
- Speak directly to the pupil rather than through a Teaching Assistant.
- Ensure access to appropriate IT equipment for the subject – and that it is used.

Scope, PO Box 833, Milton Keynes MK12 5NY
Tel: 0808 800 3333 (Freephone helpline)  Fax: 01908 321051
Email: cphelpline@scope.org.uk  Website: http://www.scope.org.uk

## Down's Syndrome (DS)

Down's Syndrome is the most common identifiable cause of learning disability. This is a genetic condition caused by the presence of an extra chromosome 21. People with DS have varying degrees of learning difficulties ranging from mild to severe. They have a specific learning profile with characteristic strengths and weaknesses. All share certain physical characteristics but will also inherit family traits in physical features and personality. They may have additional sight, hearing, respiratory and heart problems.

### Main characteristics:

- delayed motor skills
- take longer to learn and consolidate new skills
- limited concentration
- difficulties with generalisation, thinking and reasoning
- sequencing difficulties
- stronger visual than aural skills
- better social than academic skills

### How can the subject teacher help?

- Ensure that the pupil can see and hear you and other pupils.
- Speak directly to the pupil and reinforce with facial expression, pictures and objects.
- Use simple, familiar language in short sentences.
- Check instructions have been understood.
- Give time for the pupil to process information and formulate a response.
- Break lessons up into a series of shorter, varied and achievable tasks.
- Accept other ways of recording: drawings, tape/video recordings, symbols, etc.
- Set differentiated tasks linked to the work of the rest of the class.
- Provide age-appropriate resources and activities.
- Allow working in top sets to give good behaviour models.
- Provide a work buddy.
- Expect unsupported work for part of each lesson.

The Down's Association, 155 Mitcham Road, London SW17 9PG
Tel: 0845 230 0372
Email: info@downs-syndrome.org.uk
Website: http://www.downs-syndrome.org.uk

# Fragile X Syndrome

Fragile X Syndrome is caused by a malformation of the X chromosome and is the most common form of inherited learning disability. This intellectual disability varies widely, with up to a third having learning problems ranging from moderate to severe. More boys than girls are affected but both may be carriers.

## Main characteristics:

- delayed and disordered speech and language development

- difficulties with the social use of language

- articulation and/or fluency difficulties

- verbal skills better developed than reasoning skills

- repetitive or obsessive behaviour, such as hand-flapping, chewing, etc.

- clumsiness and fine motor co-ordination problems

- attention deficit and hyperactivity

- easily anxious or overwhelmed in busy environments

## How can the subject teacher help?

- Liaise with parents.

- Make sure the pupil knows what is to happen in each lesson – provide visual timetables, work schedules or written lists.

- Ensure the pupil sits at the front of the class, in the same seat for all lessons.

- Arrange a work/subject buddy.

- Where possible, keep to routines and give prior warning of all changes.

- Make instructions clear and simple.

- Use visual supports: objects, pictures, symbols.

- Allow the pupil to use a computer to record and access information.

- Give lots of praise and positive feedback.

Fragile X Society, Rood End House, 6 Stortford Road, Dunmow, Essex CM6 1DA
Tel: 01424 813147 (Helpline)  Tel: 01371 875100 (Office)
Email: info@fragilex.org.uk  Website: http://www.fragilex.org.uk

## Moderate Learning Difficulties (MLD)

The term 'moderate learning difficulties' is used to describe pupils who find it extremely difficult to achieve expected levels of attainment across the curriculum, even with a differentiated and flexible approach. These pupils do not find learning easy and can suffer from low self-esteem and sometimes exhibit unacceptable behaviour as a way of avoiding failure.

### Main characteristics:

- difficulties with reading, writing and comprehension – resulting in a particular antipathy to English as it often seems to represent all that they are bad at
- unable to understand and retain basic mathematical skills and concepts
- immature social and emotional skills
- limited vocabulary and communication skills
- short attention span
- underdeveloped co-ordination skills
- lack of logical reasoning
- inability to transfer and apply skills to different situations
- difficulty remembering what has been taught
- difficulty with organising themselves, following a timetable, remembering books and equipment

### How can the subject teacher help?

- Check the pupil's strengths, weaknesses and attainment levels.
- Establish a routine within the lesson.
- Keep tasks short and varied.
- Keep listening tasks short or broken up with activities.
- Provide word lists, writing frames, shorten text.
- Try alternative methods of recording information, e.g. drawings, charts, labelling, diagrams, use of ICT.
- Check previously gained knowledge and build on it.
- Repeat information in different ways.
- Show the child what to do or what the expected outcome is, demonstrate or show examples of completed work.
- Use practical, concrete, visual examples to illustrate explanations.
- Question the pupil to check they have grasped a concept or can follow instructions. Ask 'What do you have to do?' rather than 'Do you understand?'
- Make sure the pupil always has something to do – that the next stage is always clear
- Use lots of praise, instant rewards – catch them trying hard.

The MLD Alliance, c/o The Elfrida Society, 34 Islington Park Street, London N1 1PX
Website: www.mldalliance.com/executive.htm

# Physical Disability (PD)

There is a wide range of physical disabilities (PD), and pupils with PD cover all academic abilities. Some pupils are able to access the curriculum and learn effectively without additional educational provision. They have a disability but do not have a special educational need. For other pupils, the impact on their education may be severe, and the school will need to make adjustments to enable them to access the curriculum.

Some pupils with a physical disability have associated medical conditions which may impact on their mobility. These include cerebral palsy, heart disease, spina bifida and hydrocephalus, and muscular dystrophy. Pupils with physical disabilities may also have sensory impairments, neurological problems or learning difficulties. They may use a wheelchair and/or additional mobility aids. Some pupils will be mobile but may have significant fine motor difficulties which require support. Others may need augmentative or alternative communication aids.

Pupils with a physical disability may need to miss lessons to attend physiotherapy or medical appointments. They are also likely to become very tired as they expend greater effort to complete everyday tasks. Schools will need to be flexible and sensitive to individual pupil needs.

## How can the subject teacher help?

- Get to know pupils and parents and they will help you make the right adjustments.

- Maintain high expectations.

- Consider the classroom layout.

- Allow the pupil to leave lessons a few minutes early to avoid busy corridors and give time to get to the next lesson.

- Set homework earlier in the lesson so instructions are not missed.

- Speak directly to pupil rather than through a Teaching Assistant.

- Let pupils make their own decisions.

- Ensure access to appropriate IT equipment for the lesson – and that it is used!

- Give alternative ways of recording work.

- Plan to cover work missed through medical or physiotherapy appointments.

- Be sensitive to fatigue, especially at the end of the school day.

## Semantic Pragmatic Disorder (SPD)

Semantic Pragmatic Disorder is a communication disorder which falls within the autistic spectrum. 'Semantic' refers to the meanings of words and phrases, and 'pragmatic' refers to the use of language in a social context. Pupils with this disorder have difficulties understanding the meaning of what people say and in using language to communicate effectively. Pupils with SPD find it difficult to extract the central meaning – saliency – of situations.

### Main characteristics:

- delayed language development

- fluent speech but may sound stilted or over-formal

- may repeat phrases out of context from videos or adult conversations

- difficulty understanding abstract concepts

- limited or inappropriate use of eye contact, facial expression or gesture

- motor skills problems

### How can the subject teacher help?

- Sit the pupil at the front of the room to avoid distractions.

- Use visual supports: objects, pictures, symbols.

- Pair with a work/subject buddy.

- Create a calm working environment with clear classroom rules.

- Be specific and unambiguous when giving instructions.

- Make sure instructions are understood, especially when using subject-specific vocabulary that can have another meaning in a different context.

AFASIC, 2nd Floor, 50–52 Great Sutton Street, London EC1V 0DJ
Tel: 0845 355 5577 (Helpline 11am–2pm)  Tel: 020 7490 9410  Fax: 020 7251 2834
Email: info@afasic.org.uk  Website: http://www.afasic.org.uk

## Sensory impairments

Pupils with sensory impairments include those with varying degrees of hearing and visual difficulties, and those with multi-sensory impairment.

## Hearing impairment (HI)

The term 'hearing impairment' is a generic term used to describe all hearing loss. The main types of loss are monaural, conductive, sensory and mixed loss. The degree of hearing loss is described as mild, moderate, severe or profound. Some children rely on lip-reading, others will use hearing aids, and a small proportion will have British Sign Language (BSL) as their primary means of communication.

### How can the subject teacher help?

- Check the degree of loss the pupil has.

- Check the best seating position (e.g. away from the hum of OHP, computers, with good ear to speaker).

- Check that the pupil can see your face for facial expressions and lip reading.

- Provide a list of vocabulary, context and visual clues, especially for new subjects.

- During class discussion allow one pupil to speak at a time and indicate where the speaker is.

- Check that any aids are working and if there is any other specialist equipment available.

- Make sure the light falls on your face and lips. Do not stand with your back to a window.

- If you use interactive whiteboards, ensure that the beam does not prevent the pupil from seeing your face.

- Ban small talk.

Royal Institute for the Deaf (RNID), 19–23 Featherstone Street, London EC1Y 8SL
Tel: 0808 808 0123
British Deaf Association (BDA) 1–3 Worship Street, London ECZA 2AB
British Association of Teachers of the Deaf (BATOD), The Orchard, Leven,
North Humberside, HU17 5QA
Website: www.batod.org.uk

## Visual impairment (VI)

Visual impairment refers to a range of difficulties, including those experienced by pupils with monocular vision (vision in one eye), those who are partially sighted and those who are blind. Pupils with visual impairment cover the whole ability range and some pupils may have other SEN.

## How can the subject teacher help?

- Check the optimum position for the pupil, e.g. for a monocular pupil their good eye should be towards the action.

- Always provide the pupil with their own copy of the text.

- Provide enlarged print copies of written text.

- Check use of ICT (enlarged icons, talking text, teach keyboard skills).

- Do not stand with your back to the window as this creates a silhouette and makes it harder for the pupil to see you.

- Draw the pupil's attention to displays – which they may not notice.

- Make sure the floor is kept free of clutter.

- Tell the pupil if there is a change to the layout of a space.

- Ask if there is any specialist equipment available (enlarged print dictionaries, lights, talking scales).

Royal National Institute of the Blind, 105 Judd Street, London WC1H 9NE
Tel: 020 7388 1266  Fax: 020 7388 2034
Website: http://www.rnib.org.uk

## Multi-sensory impairment (MSI)

Pupils with multi-sensory impairment have a combination of visual and hearing difficulties. They may also have other additional disabilities that make their situation complex. A pupil with these difficulties is likely to have a high level of individual support.

### How can the subject teacher help?

- The subject teacher will need to liaise with support staff to ascertain the appropriate provision within each subject.

- Consideration will need to be given to alternative means of communication.

- Be prepared to be flexible and to adapt tasks, targets and assessment procedures.

## Severe learning difficulties (SLD)

This term covers a wide and varied group of pupils who have significant intellectual or cognitive impairments. Many have communication difficulties and/or sensory impairments in addition to more general cognitive impairments. They may also have difficulties in mobility, co-ordination and perception. Some pupils may use signs and symbols to support their communication and understanding. Their attainments may be within or below level 1 of the National Curriculum, or in the upper P scale range (P4–P8), for much of their school careers.

### How can the subject teacher help?

- Liaise with parents.

- Arrange a work/subject buddy.

- Use visual supports: objects, pictures, symbols.

- Learn some signs relevant to the subject.

- Allow time for the pupil to process information and formulate responses.

- Set differentiated tasks linked to the work of the rest of the class.

- Set achievable targets for each lesson or module of work.

- Accept different recording methods: drawings, audio or video recordings, photographs, etc.

- Give access to computers where appropriate.

- Give a series of short, varied activities within each lesson.

## Profound and multiple learning difficulties (PMLD)

Pupils with profound and multiple learning difficulties have complex learning needs. In addition to very severe learning difficulties, pupils have other significant difficulties, such as physical disabilities, sensory impairments or severe medical conditions. Pupils with PMLD require a high level of adult support, both for their learning needs and for their personal care.

They are able to access the curriculum through sensory experiences and stimulation. Some pupils communicate by gesture, eye pointing or symbols, others by very simple language. Their attainments are likely to remain in the early P scale range (P1–P4) throughout their school careers (that is below level 1 of the National Curriculum). The P scales provide small, achievable steps to monitor progress. Some pupils will make no progress or may even regress because of associated medical conditions. For this group, experiences are as important as attainment.

### How can the subject teacher help?

- Liaise with parents and Teaching Assistants.

- Consider the classroom layout.

- Identify possible sensory experiences in your lessons.

- Use additional sensory supports: objects, pictures, fragrances, music, movements, food, etc.

- Take photographs to record experiences and responses.

- Set up a work/subject buddy rota for the class.

- Identify times when the pupil can work with groups.

MENCAP, 117–123 Golden Lane, London EC1Y 0RT
Tel: 020 7454 0454  Website: http://www.mencap.org.uk

# SPECIFIC LEARNING DIFFICULTIES (SpLD)

The term 'specific learning difficulties' covers dyslexia, dyscalculia and dyspraxia.

## Dyslexia

The term 'dyslexia' is used to describe a learning difficulty associated with words, and can affect a pupil's ability to read, write and/or spell. Research has shown that there is no one definitive definition of dyslexia or one identified cause, and it has a wide range of symptoms. Although found across a whole range of ability levels, the idea that dyslexia presents as a difficulty between expected outcomes and performance is widely held.

## Main characteristics:

- The pupil may frequently lose their place while reading, make a lot of errors with the high frequency words, have difficulty reading names, and have difficulty blending sounds and segmenting words. Reading requires a great deal of effort and concentration.

- The pupils' work may seem messy with crossing outs, similarly shaped letters may be confused, such as b/d/p/q, m/w, n/u, and letters in words may be jumbled, such as tired/tried. Spelling difficulties often persist into adult life and these pupils become reluctant writers.

## How can the subject teacher help?

- Be aware of the type of difficulty and the pupil's strengths.

- Teach and allow the use of word processing, spell checkers and computer-aided learning packages.

- Provide word lists and photocopies of copying from the board.

- Consider alternative recording methods, e.g. pictures, plans, flow charts, mind maps.

- Allow extra time for tasks, including assessments and examinations.

The British Dyslexia Association
Tel: 0118 966 8271  Website: www.bda-dyslexia.org.uk
Dyslexia Institute
Tel: 07184 222300  Website: www.dyslexia-inst.org.uk

## Dyscalculia

The term 'dyscalculia' is used to describe a difficulty in mathematics. This might be either a marked discrepancy between the pupil's developmental level and general ability on measures of specific maths ability, or a total inability to abstract or consider concepts and numbers.

### Main characteristics:

- The pupil may have difficulty counting by rote, writing or reading numbers, miss out or reverse numbers, have difficulty with mental maths, and be unable to remember concepts, rules and formulae.
- In maths based concepts, the pupil may have difficulty with money, telling the time, with directions, right and left, with sequencing events or may lose track of turns, e.g. in team games, dance.

### How can the subject teacher help?

- Provide number/word/rule/formulae lists and photocopies of copying from the board.
- Make use of ICT and teach the use of calculators.
- Encourage the use of rough paper for working out.
- Plan the setting out of work with it well spaced on the page.
- Provide practical objects that are age appropriate to aid learning.
- Allow extra time for tasks including assessments and examinations.

Website: www.dyscalculia.co.uk

## Dyspraxia

The term 'dyspraxia' is used to describe an immaturity with the way in which the brain processes information, resulting in messages not being properly transmitted.

### Main characteristics:

- difficulty in co-ordinating movements, may appear awkward and clumsy
- difficulty with handwriting and drawing, throwing and catching
- difficulty following sequential events, e.g. multiple instructions
- may misinterpret situations, take things literally
- limited social skills which results in frustration and irritability
- some articulation difficulties

### How can the subject teacher help?

- Be sensitive to the pupil's limitations in games and outdoor activities and plan tasks to enable success.
- Ask the pupil questions to check his understanding of instructions/tasks.
- Check seating position to encourage good presentation (both feet resting on the floor, desk at elbow height and ideally with a sloping surface to work on).

Website: www.dyspraxiafoundation.org.uk

## Speech, language and communication difficulties (SLCD)

Pupils with SLCD have problems understanding what others say and/or making others understand what they say. Speech and language difficulties are very common in young children but most problems are resolved during the primary years. Problems that persist beyond the transfer to secondary school will be more severe. Any problem affecting speech, language and communication will have a significant effect on a pupil's self-esteem, and personal and social relationships. The development of literacy skills is also likely to be affected. Even where pupils learn to decode, they may not understand what they have read. Sign language gives pupils an additional method of communication.

Pupils with speech, language and communication difficulties cover the whole range of academic abilities.

### Main characteristics:

- Pupils who have difficulties with expressive language may experience problems in articulation and the production of speech sounds, or in co-ordinating the muscles that control speech. They may have a stammer or some other form of dysfluency.

- Pupils with receptive language impairments have difficulty understanding the meaning of what others say. They may use words incorrectly with inappropriate grammatical patterns, have a reduced vocabulary, or find it hard to recall words and express ideas. Some pupils will also have difficulty using and understanding eye-contact, facial expression, gesture and body language.

### How can the subject teacher help?

- Talk to parents, speech therapist, and the pupil about effective strategies which the school might share.
- Learn the most common signs for your subject.
- Use visual supports: objects, pictures, symbols.
- Use the pupil's name when addressing them.
- Give one instruction at a time, using short, simple sentences.
- Give time to respond before repeating a question.
- Make sure pupils understand what they have to do before starting a task.
- Pair with a work/subject buddy.
- Give access to a computer or other IT equipment appropriate to the subject.
- Give written homework instructions.

ICAN, 4 Dyer's Buildings, Holborn, London EC1N 2QP
Tel: 0845 225 4071
Email: info@ican.org.uk  Website: http://www.ican.org.uk
AFASIC, 2nd Floor, 50–52 Great Sutton Street, London EC1V 0DJ
Tel: 0845 355 5577 (Helpline 11am–2pm)  Tel: 020 7490 9410  Fax: 020 7251 2834
Email: info@afasic.org.uk  Website: http://www.afasic.org.uk

## Tourette's Syndrome (TS)

Tourette's Syndrome is a neurological disorder characterised by tics. Tics are involuntary, rapid or sudden movements or sounds that are frequently repeated. There is a wide range of severity of the condition with some people having no need to seek medical help while others have a socially disabling condition. The tics can be suppressed for a short time but will be more noticeable when the pupil is anxious or excited.

## Main characteristics:

### Physical tics

Physical tics range from simple blinking or nodding through more complex movements to more extreme conditions such as echopraxia (imitating actions seen) or copropraxia (repeatedly making obscene gestures).

### Vocal tics

Vocal tics may be as simple as throat clearing or coughing but can progress to be as extreme as echolalia (the repetition of what was last heard) or coprolalia (the repetition of obscene words).

TS itself causes no behavioural or educational problems but other, associated disorders such as Attention Deficit Hyperactivity Disorder (ADHD) or Obsessive Compulsive Disorder (OCD) may be present.

## How can the subject teacher help?

- Establish a rapport with the pupil. Find out about their interests – engage them as they enter the lesson.

- Talk to the parents in order to share strategies and establish common ground. The parents may have effective strategies which the school may not have thought of!

- Agree an 'escape route' signal (could be a hand signal or the holding up of a special card) should the tics become disruptive.

- Allow pupil to sit at the back of the room to prevent staring.

- Give access to a computer to reduce handwriting and help foster pride in presentation.

- Make sure pupil is not teased or bullied.

- Be alert for signs of anxiety or depression.

Tourette's Syndrome (UK) Association
PO Box 26149, Dunfermline, KY12 7YU
Tel: 0845 458 1252 (Helpline)  Tel: 01383 629600 (Admin)  Fax: 01383 629609
Email: enquiries@tsa.org.uk  Website: http://www.tsa.org.uk

# The Inclusive English Classroom

How do you make your classroom truly inclusive? One problem for any subject teacher can be their very expertise. It can be very hard to understand the difficulties encountered by some pupils when your own subject comes so easily to you. Whether these difficulties are to do with understanding, communicating, reading and/or writing, they can require a huge amount of effort on the part of a pupil who is trying to succeed.

## The students' point of view

An even bigger challenge is presented by the student who is starting to give up. Perhaps the first thing we should do is ask the students themselves what helps and what hinders their learning. I reproduce the findings of my current school when students were asked the pertinent questions. From their responses, we may discover many things that affect all pupils with SEN.

Here is a summary of the main points made by four different Year 11 groups:

**TABLE 4.1 RESOURCES: YEAR 11 COMMENTS**

| | |
|---|---|
| What kind of handouts/worksheets do you learn from best? | • Spacious, clearly structured<br>• Not too much text, involving a process – not just passive copying/reading<br>• Something you can keep for later revision |
| How could staff make their printed materials easier to understand? | • Improve print quality<br>• Text is often too small<br>• Examples, brief model answers<br>• Dislike 'tatty' textbooks<br>• Avoid meaningless cartoons |
| Are there any special features on worksheets that are particularly useful? | • Use bullet points and short paragraphs<br>• Highlight key words |

**TABLE 4.2  CONCEPTS: YEAR 11 COMMENTS**

| | |
|---|---|
| How do some teachers make their ideas clear and easy to follow? | • Auditory *and* visual input important<br>• Break topics into smaller units<br>• Interaction with class – constant checking of understanding<br>• Provide relevant page references |
| What do these teachers do to explain their ideas? | • Provide glossary of relevant words<br>• Emphasise vocabulary as we go along, not retrospectively<br>• Have somewhere to note down new vocabulary<br>• Write spellings of new words on board |

**TABLE 4.3  WRITING: YEAR 11 COMMENTS**

| | |
|---|---|
| How do some teachers help you to and exactly what is required in your writing? | • Specific feedback on strengths know weaknesses in their comments<br>• Demonstrate what is required<br>• Split task into manageable sections<br>• Stop a video at important points so that notes can be made (avoids the need to watch and make notes *at the same time*) |
| What guidelines and support do they give you? | • Checklists – helping to ensure everything is included<br>• Writing frames are helpful (see Appendices 4.9–4.15) |

**TABLE 4.4  READING: YEAR 11 COMMENTS**

| | |
|---|---|
| How do some teachers make reading easier? | • You read, teacher re-reads and emphasises key points<br>• Teacher uses questions and answers to recap on important points |
| What skills have they taught you to read more successfully? | • Most were not conscious of having been taught specific skills such as skimming and scanning |

The important point is that all students can give this sort of informed feedback and not just those who we consider able and articulate. Students with behaviour difficulties can also give invaluable insight into their appropriate handling. Year 10 student, Wayne, has ADHD and these are his own recommendations on how to deal with him:

### TABLE 4.5 RECOMMENDATIONS OF AN ADHD STUDENT

| | |
|---|---|
| Give clear choices | I'll know where I stand and it will remind me of what might happen to me if I carry on doing what I am doing |
| Give me 'take-up' time | Time for me to follow the instruction without losing face |
| Recognise and praise when I am getting it right | But discreetly – I've got to think about my 'street cred'. I like merit stickers though |
| Don't shout | I'll just shout back and then I end up getting into deep trouble |

## Speaking and listening

These are areas of the English curriculum which can be the most difficult for children with SEN, and yet successful involvement here can provide the necessary background to successful reading and writing. It must be remembered that for some otherwise able students, this area may be a specific special need. Students often lack the necessary vocabulary to put their thoughts into words and are scared of expressing a point of view in a clumsy way.

Some students may react by ridiculing the contributions of others. Start by emphasising that your classroom is a 'No Put Down' zone. Where I teach, this is accompanied by large 'No Entry' style signs with the 'No Put Down Zone' across the middle. Forgetful students are therefore instantly reminded of this particular classroom creed.

Establish also that all contributions have to go through the chair – which might be you, but on occasion might be a student. This provides practice in turn-taking and reinforces an ethos of valuing everybody's contribution. (See Appendix 4.1 for a simple reminder about turn taking – basics which may have to be explicitly taught to some students, e.g. those with ASD.) Establish other ground rules associated with putting hands up. Phrase questions that involve the words 'how', 'why', 'when', 'where', 'who', 'what would happen if . . .'? Two techniques for questioning are outlined below.

### Snowball technique

This technique, as outlined by Robert Powell (1997), can be particularly helpful for shy students. The idea is to put pupils into ever larger groups in order to share and build on ideas. For example:

- The teacher could start by asking the question, 'Why did the fight break out between the Montagues and the Capulets?'

- The students have one minute in silence to think of as many reasons as they can to answer this.

- Then they work for two minutes in pairs exchanging their ideas with a partner.

- The pairs then form groups of four, exchanging ideas and thinking of two new ones.

- In the information-gathering sessions the teacher takes one idea from each group to ensure a greater chance of maximum participation.

The advantage for the SEN student is there is far greater likelihood of oral participation.

## Post-it note technique

This is another excellent Powell technique and it has the additional advantage of being very simple to operate. An example of an adjective or an adverb or other type of word is written on the post-it and placed on the forehead of a volunteer. The audience is only allowed to answer 'yes' or 'no' to the questions the volunteer asks. Powell got the idea from Mark Jones of Forres Academy, and cites the following benefits of this technique:

- It develops thinking skills.

- It encourages students to use logic in order to solve the problem. Students have to listen carefully.

- It develops the ability to recall key knowledge quickly.

- It is a useful way of re-visiting key vocabulary and language.

- It is fun – and I might add that it works! You may find it quite surprising how the most reticent student engages in this process.

- It obviously lends itself to more complex ideas, such as exploring a character in a novel or a play.

- It could be used to identify a poem in an anthology. The Post-it could read 'Digging' by Seamus Heaney. The teacher could extend the questioning, preventing the volunteer asking, 'Is it 'Digging?' too soon by scoring him or her on the number of 'yes' responses they get to the questions. Of course, for many weaker students, getting the response 'Digging' will be enormously rewarding in itself. Their understanding of the poem can then be developed by further discussion about how they arrived at their decision.

## Receptive language difficulties

There are significant numbers of pupils in secondary schools who have problems in understanding what is said to them. Often, they are thought to be badly behaved, unco-operative and/or poor listeners when the problem actually lies in their lack of understanding. It will benefit these pupils (and all pupils in the class) if the teacher adopts the following strategies:

● Ensure that instructions are clear and unambiguous: 'I want you to listen very carefully while I read the poem, and follow it on your sheet. Then I will ask you to highlight some of the words used in a particular way – I'll explain that after the reading . . .'

● Explain unfamiliar vocabulary and any newly introduced terminology: 'Swarupa, I want you to be the narrator – that's the person who tells, or reads the story.'

● Check regularly for pupils' understanding: 'Can you go over what you have to do, Shaun, just to remind everyone . . .' (The teacher will judge whether this tactic is appropriate or whether it will put Shaun 'on the spot' – in which case, a quiet word one-to-one might be better.)

● Avoid speaking too quickly and allow time for pupils to 'take in' what you have said: a few seconds can seem a long time to the teacher, and to quick-thinking members of the class, but not to a youngster with language difficulties. It may be useful to say something like, 'Think about that, Jordan, and you can tell us our answer in a few moments.' (He might prepare a response with the help of a Teaching Assistant.)

● Say the pupil's name before asking the question, to alert him and ensure he is paying attention. Make sure he is looking at you and can see your face so that he can pick up non-verbal cues (also important for pupils with hearing impairment).

● Use visual aids, where possible, to reinforce the spoken word, e.g. symbol cards to convey the level of noise you expect at any time (complete silence, quiet voices for group discussion or pair work, loud voice for speaking up to the class, etc.)

## Expressive language problems

Difficulties with expressing thoughts and ideas may go hand-in-hand with receptive language problems, or occur even when pupils' understanding of language is good. Problems with word finding and sequencing can combine to make the pupil so nervous and tense that his difficulties are exacerbated in front of his classmates. Teachers can help by:

- allowing thinking time rather than expecting an immediate answer: 'Matthew, how do we know that Macbeth felt bad about killing Duncan? Let's all think about that for a moment and put together a good answer in our heads . . .';

- encouraging pupils to practise in pairs before speaking to a group or the whole class;

- building in 'rehearsal time' for oral presentation of project work etc;

- making use of puppets and role play when appropriate: this can give pupils confidence and take away some of their nervousness;

- providing structure for responses and presentations, such as the use of 'talking frames' (see Appendix 4.2).

## Stammering

Stammering is not very common, but can result in a lot of embarrassment and suffering for pupils whose speech is variable and unpredictable. It can be particularly debilitating in English, where speaking is such an important element of the curriculum.

Teachers need to be aware of the challenges facing a child who stammers, and do as much as possible to understand and support him. Stammering is a very variable condition, and if the pupil is worried and anxious it will always be worse than if he is relaxed and confident.

---

**A NEGATIVE SITUATION**

Pupil thinks: 'I am bound to stammer over this and they will laugh at me' → feels embarrassed → becomes tense → avoids having to speak, or tries to speak but stammers badly.

**A POSITIVE SITUATION**

Pupil thinks: 'Everyone is used to me and no one will laugh if I stammer' → feels confident → is relaxed → speaks more fluently with less stammering.

---

*Figure 4.1*

It is important for the teacher to set the standard in responding to a pupil who stammers – providing a model for other pupils to follow. You can help by:

- being understanding and patient;

- asking the pupil who can help;

- allowing preparation time;

- giving him time to finish;

- avoiding putting him under a lot of pressure;

- helping him to use words that are simple to say;

- building up his confidence.

## Reading texts: classroom strategies

Why are there still some students who can't read properly when they reach secondary school? There are many books and theories on this, and a mistake that many secondary SENCOs have made in the past is somehow assuming that the primary schools have got it all wrong and that they will manage to create excellent readers where the primaries have failed. However, the IEPs that accompany students from primary school often tell a story of extremely hard work on the part of all concerned.

It is essential that this work is built on in the secondary school. There needs to be close co-operation between the SENCO and the English department so that techniques used in any 'catch-up' programme are understood and not under-mined by classroom practice. English teachers need to build on any learning success achieved in small-group or one-to-one work.

### So what can you do in your classroom?

- You could establish a short, regular reading time (no more than ten minutes) at the beginning of each English lesson and use this for yourself and your TA to hear weaker readers read. Students could bring in their own books. I also keep a small selection of 'quick reads' in the classroom, from which they may choose if they wish.

- How good a reader are *you*? There is still a place for reading aloud to a class, and a skilful reader can really bring a text alive. Try using different accents, or, failing that, a higher or lower register to your voice to indicate different characters.

- You could share the reading with a TA. Just having two voices dealing with a text can make it 'live' a little more. Reading a book like *Stone Cold* by Robert Swindells particularly lends itself to this. I was lucky enough to have a particularly menacing sounding TA to take on the role of 'Shelter', but even a flat monotone would be appropriate here!

- Stop at regular intervals to recap on key events and ideas. Check pupils' understanding of less familiar vocabulary.

- Peer support should be encouraged, although students should not be allowed to jump in to 'help' too quickly. Jenny can help Jimmy by prompting a word when he needs it. If Jimmy is trying some independent reading this is *all* Jenny needs to do. She should not be drawn in to 'sounding-it-out' or other such techniques. That is best left to the class teacher or TA.

- If your school has a sixth form, fantastic use can be made of their in-class support. Confident sixth-formers could take pairs or small groups of students out of the class to read aloud to them or to read short extracts from, for example, a Shakespeare play.

- You could set up a reading group of older students (not necessarily sixth formers) who undertake to read texts onto tape. This can be a valuable experience for the readers too, especially drama students. Walkman type tape recorders and headphones can be obtained quite cheaply from specialist independent suppliers, such as 'ianSYST', who vet the products they sell and also give good advice.

- There are many taped books available from the BBC and other sources (e.g. Smartpass), and their use should be actively encouraged by the English department and the library, and not just for students with reading difficulties. Hearing a good story read by an actor such as Timothy West can be a rich experience for anybody, and can help to make classic literature accessible. Able dyslexics can especially benefit from these. This is a particularly useful strategy for helping students to study set texts for GCSEs.

- The use of video can also be motivating (for all pupils, but especially those with ADHD, ASD and MLD) and helps to maintain interest, increase under-standing and speed up the rate at which pupils can work through a book.

- You can use skilful readers in the class to take the part of different characters. (I feel that this procedure should always be voluntary.)

- One problem for all English departments is how to get their students off an endless diet of *Goosebumps* and *Point Horror*. Turner and Pughe (2003) in their book *English and Dyslexia* describe an excellent Reading Passport Scheme in which students have to get their passport stamped by sampling a magazine, a Welsh author, a book of poetry, a non-fiction book about animals or sport, and so on. This is an excellent means of getting all students to experience different genres. You might want to consider keeping an accessible selection of these available in a class book box, to support your weaker or less enthusiastic readers. Make sure there are plenty of 'quick reads' available (rather than books termed 'easy reads').

## What should you do if a known poor reader volunteers to read?

- *Do not* pass them over. Tell the pupil which passage they will be asked to read so that they can look at it (or even practise it) beforehand. This can be useful homework.

- Ask them to read a shorter passage and tell them that you would like them to read again in a few minutes, if they want to read more. That way, you keep the pace of the text moving and maintain the interest of the rest of the class. Your weaker readers are also less likely to stumble over a short passage and will feel more satisfied with their own performance.

- With drama texts, find a comparatively undemanding part for them.

- Once again, peer support can help them to keep their place and give them suitable prompts.

- They could also use an excellent, unobtrusive device from Crossbow education (see website) which can help them keep their place on a line. It is a flexible, translucent plastic strip which can be laid on the paper. It is also a great help for those with a tendency to scotopic sensitivity.

*Remember that pupils who are weak readers need to practise more, not less.*

Many schools have facilities for pupils to spend some time during the lunch break, or before first lesson, in a comfy room or library area, reading books or listening to tapes. This is often staffed by a TA, but occasional visits from an English teacher will provide valuable encouragement and support.

## Reading for learning

This is what the experience can be like for a poor reader:
- Sometimes key          are omitted
- Sometimes other words or letters      omitted
- Sometimes we think a word means its opposite.
                and
- Some letters      words appear in th  line above.
                                        e
- or below
- Sometimes words or letters are umjlbed up in a line.
- Sometimes the text is completely reversed as in a rorrim.
- Sometimes we can read a word on one page but not      the next.
- In any case we often have to read every single letter more or less as you are doing now but you are much better than us because you can guess the word before the end of it. Often we do not get to the end before the teacher goes on to

*Figure 4.2*

## Material

It can be surprising – and alarming – to discover that pupils are able to read aloud without actually understanding much of the text. This happens more commonly than you may think with students who have special educational needs. An example of this occurred in a lesson with a Year 10 group who were asked to complete a simple cloze exercise, including the sentence: 'The king was crowned ___ Westminster Abbey.' The gap was filled with: 'in', 'at', 'on', 'with' and 'by'.

If you hear individual pupils read aloud and then question them carefully about what they have 'read', you may well find a significant lack of understanding. Sometimes, the reader has concentrated so hard on 'de-coding' that he has failed to convert the text to meaning. This can also happen with competent readers, of course – we have all read to the end of a page and realised that our minds have been somewhere else! With pupils who are still developing as readers, however, it is important to address this issue. (See Appendix 4.3 'The Furbles of Tarp', for an example of how a comprehension exercise can be completed without any comprehension at all!)

Introduce the text – set the scene, ask pupils to predict what might happen and clarify new vocabulary. Here are some more suggestions:

- After reading – paraphrase, summarise, use careful questioning.

- Re-read – this gives readers an opportunity to practise the art of reading aloud, with expression, and allows an 'extra bite of the cherry' in terms of understanding the text, both for the reader and those listening.

- Engage pupils in an activity which requires them to interact directly with the text, e.g. 'Find the sentence which tells us exactly how Tom felt'; 'Highlight all the words that give us information about the setting/weather/relationship.'

- Ask a group of pupils to prepare the text before the lesson (for homework?) and in the lesson they can introduce/read/explain/ it to the rest of the class. (This is a good activity for the TA to use in support of a small group.)

A lesson plan intended to develop predictive reading skills is given in Appendix 4.4.

## Worksheets

How clear are your worksheets? Try to look at them critically. Are they badly reproduced? I knew of a department that, for understandable reasons associated with cost, reduced all their worksheets to A5 size. This meant that quite a few words were effectively just black blobs. Again, the skilled readers could just about work out the context of the sentence, but poorer readers found it difficult to use such context clues. Check that you have used a suitable font size; if it is too small it will put off your less enthusiastic readers.

Are your worksheets old, faded or creased? Throw them out or re-vamp them. SEN students are far less likely to produce neat work if the material they are presented with is tired and messy. Get rid of any handwritten material for the same reason.

Have you checked the readability level of the text? SENCOs should be happy to advise, but the formula is very simple and can be accessed from a word-processing package like Microsoft Word:

- select *Tools*

- then *Options*

- click on the *Spelling and Grammar* tab

- select *Show readability statistics*

- click on *OK*

On the *Standard* toolbar, click *Spelling and Grammar*. When Word finishes checking spelling and grammar, it will display (in American grade level) the readability of the text.

Alternatively, you can use the 'SMOG' technique:

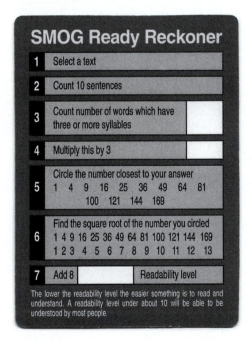

**Figure 4.3** Smog Ready Reckoner

You will, of course, need to know the reading ages or levels of the students in your group to assess any mismatch of text to reader. It is also important to remember that knowing the context of a piece of writing makes a significant difference to a reader. If a reader understands about witches and wizards and all the paraphernalia associated with them because he has listened to stories and/or watched films about them, he will be able to guess at words he has not seen in print before (besom, cauldron, elixir). It can be very useful then, to *introduce* a story, poem or play before beginning to read it – to cue in the readers to new vocabulary and concepts.

## Reading resources

Access to good literature is another issue. Your highly developed reading skills allow you access to complicated and intriguing ideas: complex characters, finely constructed plots, suspense, drama – the list goes on.

The literature available to students with a reading age of nine and below is going to be restricted in these areas. However, there is much excellent material on the market which has appropriate reading ages and has the additional benefit of being short. Michael Morpurgo, among others, writes about interesting and challenging topics in an accessible way. (See recommendations on the following page.)

The following collections are worth exploring:

- *Spirals* published by Stanley Thornes (Nelson Thornes). See: www.nelsonthornes.com
- *Sprinters* published by Walker books. See: www.walkerbooks.com
- Penguin publish a series that does a particularly good job of looking 'adult' in appearance – mirroring the sleeve design of its ordinary books. See: www.penguin.co.uk
- The Barrington Stoke series. Before publication, all the books are read by the 'customers', the reluctant readers themselves. Barrington Stoke say: 'Their comments are taken into account, and many of the children's suggested changes are made. Children and teenagers who comment on the manuscript receive a free copy of the book, and their names appear in the list of consultants at the back of the book.' All consultants need to have a reading age of 8+. You can find out how your students could become Barrington Stoke consultants by visiting their website. There are enormous English teaching benefits from doing this! See: www.barringtonstoke.co.uk
- *Livewire* series published by Hodder and Stoughton in association with the Basic Skills Agency. This is a particularly good non-fiction series of contemporary and historical biography which is being added to all the time. They also do profiles of quite a number of football teams. The text is thought provoking, particularly with regard to 'real lives' and adult in tone. They do not duck important issues such as George Best's alcoholism or Martina Navratilova's sexuality. See: www.hodder.co.uk
- *Livewire Investigates* is another series which reports on such things as 'extreme sports'. The spines are colour coded for reading age so you can direct the reader to the appropriate level without them knowing. See: www.hodder.co.uk
- Very reluctant readers can be encouraged with the use of plays such as the *Impact* plays published by Ginn. See: www.ginn.co.uk

It is vital that the use of these books comes under the umbrella of the English department and the library. It is also important that they are labelled 'Quick Reads' rather than 'Easy Reads' (avoids pejorative overtones) and that they are available to everyone. Educational psychologists regard a reading age of 9.5 as 'functional', which means that these readers have sufficient skills to survive in the outside world. However, it is obviously desirable to try and improve on this score, especially as much of the reading that children will face at secondary school will be at a higher level.

## Some other useful resources

Visual back-up is vital for many students. Storyboards, character collages and timelines will all help with developing understanding and improving pupils' recall. Classroom displays of word banks – nouns, verbs, adjectives, adverbs, etc., can also be helpful. (If you have wheelchair users in your class, remember to place displays at an appropriate height for them, as well as everybody else.)

Cutting Edge Publications of Cornwall produces excellent support materials for many of the set texts (see Appendix 4.5 for sample pages). They are cheap and photocopiable with masses of ideas for engaging students in the text while keeping to the golden rule of having just enough words on the page to direct the student to the task. The company also markets booklets which provide a synopsis of various set texts, with accompanying pictures in the same style as their study packs. These are excellent for getting an overall picture, literally, of the text to be studied. They can act as a revision aid for some students and/or form the basis of a classroom display when 'blown up' on the photocopier. These are particularly helpful, of course, for visual learners.

Another very useful Cutting Edge resource is their 'character cards' which they provide to accompany most, if not all, of their set text resources. They are excellent as writing prompts:

- Students select cards which are relevant to the topic they have to write about.

- They can therefore write from point to point.

- When they run out of ideas, the cards can help start them off again and help them to produce a sustained piece of coursework.

Some other things you can do with the character cards:

- Pick a character card. Choose one describing word from the vocabulary list. Explain how this word fits the named character.

- Same or opposite? Pick any character word. Name a character who fits this word. Name a character that would not fit this word. Explain why.

- Odd one out: Student number one collects three related cards and then adds a fourth as the odd one out. Student two has to spot the card and explain why it does not match.

- Other ideas come with each pack!

From September 2004, Cutting Edge will also have resources on audio CD.

For students studying the AQA/A poetry anthology *Poems from Different Cultures*, they have also produced a useful resource: Cutting Edge Publications, Lostwithiel, Cornwall PL22 OJR Tel: 01208 872337.

Most English departments have a shared resource bank of materials to support pupils with SEN. These can be quickly made these days with appropriate software, such as *ClozePro*, Crick software, or you could scan in a piece of text used in class and give it out for homework as a cloze exercise, or as jumbled sentences or a sequencing exercise. This is a very useful task for TAs to be helping with.

## Symbols

Teachers will increasingly be expected to teach students who have very significant needs, possibly as part of a part-time placement in a mainstream school. For these pupils, conventionally written communication may be inaccessible. In special schools and settings, symbols are used to great effect, and there is no reason why mainstream teachers should not take advantage of this alternative communication system. The symbols may simply act as a reminder of the language, but can also help to bring richer language within the grasp of pupils with SEN.

Clearly, some texts lend themselves to symbol support better than others. This poem by W. H. Auden has clear concepts which make it easy to find symbol representations which can convey meaning.

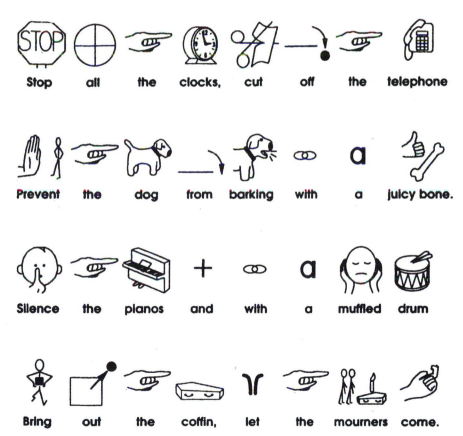

**Figure 4.4** *Word symbols*

Grove (2004), in *Ways into Literature,* shows how imaginative approaches can successfullly introduce students with severe difficulties to classical literature, and the *Inclusive Readers* series (David Fulton, 2002) has a fully supported version of *The Tempest.*

Many organisations produce their own symbol-supported materials which are circulated locally, and publications such as *Literacy Through Symbols* by Tina and Mike Detheridge and *Symbols Now* (Abbott) have helped to spread good practice. Software packages such as those provided by Widgit (www.widgit.com) make the provision of personalised resources very quick and easy – and is something a TA could help with (and also provide invaluable support for pupils' own recording). The introduction of symbols in mainstream settings is still in its infancy, but is proving to be highly effective with a range of pupils where it is used judiciously.

## Using the board

If you still have a blackboard, get it changed for a whiteboard. A considerable number of reading problems arise because students cannot read what is on the board. This may be because the board is old and chalk ingrained and the sunlight shines on it at crucial times. If you have to stick with a blackboard, insist on it being properly cleaned and/or repainted regularly. (If you do this enough times, the management team will get fed up with you and provide a whiteboard.)

Having got your whiteboard, always ensure that you have a range of colours available. Why is that that the only one you can ever find is green? Not all of your students will find this easy to read and it causes more problems when it starts to wear out. Change your board markers when they *start* to wear out. Don't wait until your writing is so faint that it is difficult to read from the back of the room. Although able, efficient readers can make sense of your faint board writing because they are able to use context clues to determine the overall meaning; poorer readers cannot do this because they have to read every word.

To get an idea of the difficulties faced by poor readers, try turning a piece of fairly complicated text upside down and then reading it. You will find you lower your reading age quite considerably! If you present a piece of text typed out back-to-front for colleagues to read, this is also an effective demonstration of how hard some pupils have to work in order to decipher the printed word. Imagine the effort needed to do this all the time. Try, for example, reading the following sentence:

!nuf hcum t'nsi yllaer tI

We often comment upon our students' handwriting, but have you looked at the readability of your own recently? Take the time to stand at the back of your classroom. How easy is it to read what you have written from there? (This is worth doing when you are presenting information on an OHP, too.) If, like mine, your handwriting becomes less legible towards the bottom of the board, then stop before you reach that point.

Even if you are a neat hand writer, you may still cause problems for your poor readers because of the way you join certain letters. For instance, words with 'r' and 'n' together will appear like an 'm' to a poor reader (think of the word 'return'). They will lack the contextual skills to work this out. In this respect, and in so many others, we can learn from our primary colleagues. Print your writing on the board and in lower case letters to give poor readers a sporting chance of deciphering the text. This might seem strange at first, but keep it up and you will get faster. I know that this would appear to fly in the face of conventional wisdom, but it is perhaps one more example of accepted practice failing to take account of the special needs of weaker readers and writers.

Use your range of colours to emphasise the structure of key words that you are going to introduce. We are now used to introducing key words at the beginning of lessons but, by using different colours within a word, you can draw attention to its key elements, for example the 'aud' bit of '*aud*ience' might be worth emphasising or 'para' in 'se*para*te'.

Last but not least, make sure that pupils with SEN, especially those with any visual impairment, are positioned appropriately so that they have a good view of the board.

## Interactive whiteboards

Interactive whiteboards are appearing in more and more classrooms, and making a positive impact. Becta has information on the Virtual Teachers Centre (VTC): *http://vtc.ngfl.gov.uk*

## Advantages

- Pupils appear to be more interested in presentations using the board.

- Teachers make wider use of a variety of media, and lessons are more 'interactive'.

- The ability to create 'movement' on the board through dragging and dropping text and pictures, or using animation in software such as PowerPoint, is valuable to kinaesthetic learners, and can aid the understanding of grammar.

- Students are keen to use this medium for their own presentations, enhancing their own oral and presentational skills.

- It is easier for all pupils to understand the processes underlying reading and writing when these skills are approached as whole-class activities via an electronic whiteboard. The focus provided by the whiteboard and the increased opportunities for interactivity with the text mean that the pupils are more fully engaged with the tasks.

- Teachers have access to a great range of resources – more than they would normally be able to use in a traditional classroom with no computer. It is useful to be able to open presentations that have already been delivered for revision purposes or to draw on a bank of resources saved on the computer or the school network.

- Transitions between different activities linked via an interactive whiteboard are smoother, as all the resources are readily to hand through a central point.

## Considerations

- Is the board positioned so that it can easily be seen by everyone in the class?

- Can pupils use the board without standing in the beam?

- Is there a child who is reliant on lip reading? If so, arrange for them to sit near the front in a position where they can see your mouth clearly. Make sure you stand where the light does not hide your face. They will need to see mouth shapes clearly if they are to have any hope of pronouncing the sounds.

- Is the text on the screen easy to read? Check the font size. Where teachers write additional notes on the screen as well, the text can become jumbled and hard to read.

- There are health and safety issues. Check cables are covered. This is especially important for pupils who are visually impaired.

## Writing

Writing is a complex task and often proves to be even more of a challenge than speaking and reading for pupils with special educational needs. It is, however, an important part of communicating, as well as a tool for thinking and learning. Unlike speaking, writing allows for revision, extension and interpolation; it helps us to plan, sort out our ideas, develop arguments and explore feelings.

Written language has different syntactic and textual characteristics from the spoken word, and there is not necessarily a connection between competencies in speaking and writing – many pupils will be able to 'spin a yarn' to entertain their friends, but struggle to compose a well-structured sentence on paper. The writer has to consider what to write, how to write it (i.e. choice of words, sentence structure) and then how to transfer the words in his head into decipherable marks on the paper (handwriting, spelling, punctuation).

For pupils with special needs, much of the time devoted to writing is often focused on developing the 'secretarial skills' of neat handwriting, correct spelling and punctuation. They may come to regard the writing process as a mechanistic and futile task rather than as a tool for thinking and working out, expressing oneself, sharing joys and sorrows, and experiencing the satisfaction of creating and sharing something unique. A good way of putting them off writing is to rush them into a writing task, with a time limit for completion and an insistence on 'best handwriting'. Adults who write for a living will tell you that these exhortations are anathema to them. In the first place you have to *want* to write and you have to have something to write *about*. Secondly, it is rare to write anything that cannot be improved by re-drafting and consultation with a 'critical friend' – preferably coming back to the work after a reasonable interval rather than in the same session/lesson.

Good preparation for writing is crucial for pupils with SEN, and can take many forms:

- reading or listening to an inspiring story, play or poem

- discussing a controversial issue

- using a picture or photo as a starting point

- brainstorming – drawing on pupils' own experiences

- making a plan, wordlist, mind map

- using artefacts as stimuli

- role play

A combination of these approaches can provide really strong motivation to write, e.g. read about an argument between parent and child; role play in pairs the continuation of the argument; one or two couples 'perform' for the rest of the class. The teacher notes down some of the key words used on the board – the pupils then set to writing – they have the ideas, the vocabulary and the personal involvement required to get going with the task.

The list in Figure 4.5 (below) offers some further ideas for supporting pupils with writing, and these activities might usefully be undertaken with a TA, where students need more time to assimilate ideas and assemble useful words, etc.

Help writers to:
- formulate and articulate their thoughts, ideas and feelings
- develop a fluid handwriting style and/or keyboard skills
- learn the spellings of high-frequency words
- hear the sounds in a word they want to write and know how to represent those sounds on paper
- make analogies – if you can spell *might*, you can also spell *fight, light, night, right*
- use what they know to problem-solve
- have the confidence to 'have a go' with new words
- understand how to learn from their mistakes
- look critically at their own work and make constructive comments about others'

Remember to:
- model the writing process (thinking aloud about how to spell words, phrase sentences: 'Is this the best word I can use?' etc.)
- provide a stimulating print-rich environment
- provide regular opportunities for all sorts of writing

**Figure 4.5** *Supporting writers*

## The stages of writing

Pupils are often in a hurry to write something down (anything will do!), or conversely, find it a mammoth task to get beyond the date and title. By breaking down the task for them and establishing a routine for writing, we can help them to produce work which they can be proud of. Figure 4.6 outlines four main stages to go through when approaching a writing task. The 'Plan, Do, Review' approach can be encouraged by providing pupils with appropriate paper/books and folders, and some tried and tested strategies are listed below:

- Use rough jotters for mapping out ideas and trying spellings, best/neat books or file paper for final product.

- Use left-side page for rough work, right side page for best.

- Use alternate lines when writing without a rough draft – this allows for insertions/corrections/amendments/ when revising.

- Use a wide margin for annotations.

- Use folders and loose-leaf paper so that only best work is kept and pupils start each new project with a 'clean sheet'.

## Spelling

All our spelling ages are likely to be lower than our reading ages and it is important to realise that spelling is a visual, not an auditory, skill. Test the following words out on unsuspecting colleagues (from Charles Cripps' training materials):

> liaison, benefited, permanent, separate, gauge, pedlar, focused, cemetery

The chances are that at least some of them will get a few of them wrong. Confident spellers, which most English teachers are, will be horrified if they have made a mistake. I know of at least one person who went to check in a dictionary, such was their disbelief! This has the double advantage of making them feel as uncomfortable as some of our students, as well as demonstrating that we can all do with help with spelling whatever our age and ability, and that we can read many more words than we can comfortably spell. If we really want to create an inclusive classroom we must provide as much support for spelling as we can.

It really matters to most students that they get the word right and, in my experience, it is the main reason why some students are reluctant to begin the process of writing.

### How can you provide support?

- Use key words at the beginning of the lesson. 'Print' them on the board and draw attention to the structure of them, e.g. the man in per*man*ent, the para in se*para*te.

# THE FOUR STAGES OF WRITING

**Thinking**

What to write (see list at bottom)
- what order to do things in (make a plan or mind map; beginning-middle-end; paragraph headings; subtitles)

How to prepare in your head
- (by talking things through, on paper if it is complicated)

Where to research
- If you need to find things out before you write: (make up some questions you need to answer, look in books, or on the internet, ask other people, make observations)

**First draft**

In jotter or on rough paper

**Revising**

Writing often needs re-drafting. The changes you make will result in your work becoming more clear, more interesting, more concise or more powerful.

Ask yourself:
- Are things in the right order?
- Do all the sentences mean what I want them to mean?
- Does every word count? Can anything be cut out?
- Are the words well chosen? Can I think of any which are more interesting, more accurate or more unusual?
- Have I repeated the same word, or said the same thing twice, without meaning to?
- Is it legible?
- Is it interesting?
- Have I checked spelling and punctuation?

It is always better to revise your work after a break. Come back to it the next day if possible – you will see it with new eyes and find it easier to make a good assessment. Get someone else to read it and say what they think (if you're brave enough) – or read it aloud to them.

**Final version**

This is not just a neater copy of the first draft.

story (narrative), notes, letter (to complain, explain, enquire, persuade), report, list, instructions, explanation, description, discussion, factual record, poem, diary, pamphlet, news item, recipe, play, eye-witness account, interview, debate, argument, biography, autobiography

*Figure 4.6 The four stages of writing*

- Colour code the difficult bits. To get pupils used to the routine, choose a word like 'disappearance' and see how many words they can find within it, e.g. *is, sap, pear, ran.* The rules are that they can use the letters as many times as they like but they cannot change the order of the letters.

- Get the students used to the idea that when they want a spelling you will write it down for them rather than spelling it out verbally. This can be in a personal spelling book or the middle pages (where the staples are) of an exercise book. The latter idea has the advantage that when the book is full you can remove the middle pages and they can be placed in a new book or in a folder which houses other subject-specific words.

- It is always worth encouraging a pupil to 'have a go' on a scrap of paper before you provide a correct spelling. They will often get it right – or 'nearly right' (never 'wrong'!) – especially if you give them the appropriate number of blank spaces in the way that is done for a game of Hangman.

- If a pupil regularly uses a word processor, it might be worth demonstrating how to set up a word bank on the computer. If this is done in Word then it can appear as a window on the screen which can be called up while they are working on a piece of writing. When errors are highlighted, they can transfer the correct spelling to their word bank. (See below.)

- In any spare moment, by themselves or preferablywith a partner, children can practise the meaning and the spelling of their words using the LOOK-COVER-WRITE-CHECK routine. Alternatively, it could occupy the first or last five minutes of a lesson.

Get the students used to the routine of checking their word bank for a word, whether on computer or in their books, before they ask you. This is particularly helpful for the student who persistently gets the same word wrong, and has the double advantage of acting as a constant reinforcement. The basic principle of LOOKING at the word, SAYING it (in a quiet voice in a crowded classroom), COVERING it, WRITING it from memory and CHECKING that you have got it right has not been bettered.

This technique should (eventually) commit the word visually into the long-term memory. It may serve to demonstrate how many times a group of spellings might need reinforcing! As a refinement, the students could highlight the bit that has proved difficult for them, using a classroom highlighter pen, a yellow felt pen or a yellow crayon. You have, incidentally, a ready-made source of homework here.

Students with vastly different levels of spelling will nevertheless label themselves poor spellers. Confidence is a major factor, and I have found that the following system gives a fair degree of empowerment to weak or fearful spellers:

- Many spelling mistakes that students make *will only involve one or two letter errors* and will often involve vowels. Some students will feel empowered if you identify the mistake by underlining it and using the following code placed in the margin:

- +1 = one letter too many. (e.g. whent)

- −1 = one letter is missing. (e.g. lerning)

- ×1 = one letter is wrong. (e.g. irgent)

- This code may be used for errors involving two letters where they occur together in a word (e.g. −2: rember for rem*em*ber).

- If you find this procedure too time-consuming in practice, restrict yourself to five words – preferably words that you are using frequently in your subject.

- More complicated spelling errors may be indicated by writing the word out and highlighting or emphasising the difficult bit (e.g. 'w*or*d' or 'w<u>or</u>d').

This is still a worthwhile practice even when there are other *complicated* errors, as the student may still feel that they are dealing with their own problems. It should be a matter of departmental policy to decide just how many words you would identify in a single piece of work. To mark every spelling can be counter-productive. It goes without saying that this is a strategy that can benefit all students and should not be a means of singling out those for whom spelling is a significant problem. Appendix 4.6 suggests a format for a departmental meeting to determine the design of key word books and to formulate a spelling policy.

Obviously your cause and that of the SEN Learning Support department would be helped if you used a departmental policy as a basis for setting up a whole-school policy on spelling.

Examinations for students with learning difficulties can be a double-edged sword. Many SENCOs feel that GCSE has moved further and further away from being accessible to students with SEN, and yet there have never before been so many enabling devices which can be so beneficial to them. Apart from a huge number of specific programmes geared to help spelling, there is a lot that can be done with word-processor programs such as Microsoft Word.

The information in Figure 4.7 describes a process that can be used both at home and at school and may be constantly updated. In effect, the student is using the computer as a glorified spell-checker, but one which can directly support word-processed work, and indeed hand-written work, if the computer is close by.

Students can also make use of the Track Changes facility on 'Tools'. If this is switched on when they begin the process of spell-checking they can have an on-going record of the precise corrections they have made and, therefore, a specific spelling list to work from.

The British Educational Communications Technology Association [BECTa] summarises the advantages of using ICT to support students' writing, claiming it:

- affords the privacy to work and develop at the learner's own pace

- encourages all students to work independently, creating opportunities for making the best use of human resources.

# Using computers to support the spelling and meaning of key words

The aim is to make a list of words that you use frequently in the different subjects that you study. This method should help you to remember the spelling and the meaning of the words. It should also help you with your revision for your exams.

Here is the step by step guide:

- Type the word onto the screen.

- If and when the red squiggly line appears, place the cursor on top of the word and click the RIGHT hand mouse button. Even if the word turns out to be correct, keep it on your list. The important thing to remember is that you were unsure about it!

- A list of possible correct spellings will appear on the screen.

- Clicking on the word you want will result in an instant correction.

- Highlight/*italicise*/**bold** the difficult bits of the word and then add them to your list. Click the 'buttons' on the formatting toolbar; the one with **B** / <u>U</u> on it.

- The highlighter command is the one before the letter <u>A</u> on the right hand side of this toolbar.

Use the sort command to put the words into alphabetical order:

- Hold down the 'Control ' button and press the letter A . The whole document will be highlighted .

- Click on 'Table' at the top of the screen. Move the cursor down to 'Sort'.

- Click again, and the whole list of words will be put into alphabetical order.

- Now write the meaning beside it if you think it is necessary. If there is any doubt about this – then do it!

**Figure 4.7** *Using a spell-checker*

Every classroom should also have a number of ACE spelling dictionaries by David Moseley (published by LDA Associates). This is a phonic-based dictionary where students look up words on the basis of how the word sounds. Think how demoralising it must be to be told to look up the word 'urgent' when it could just as easily begin with the letters 'er' or 'ir'.

This is a dictionary which students will either love or hate, but there are sufficient numbers of those who really struggle with spelling and who see this remarkable dictionary as invaluable to justify an English department strategically placing five of these dictionaries in each classroom. The process needs some practice, but do not attempt to judge its effectiveness from your own (effective speller) standpoint. You really need to trial it on a number of phonetic (possibly dyslexic), spellers to gain a true impression of its usefulness. Dyslexia often (but by no means always) runs in families, so eliciting the help of a self-confessed or closet dyslexic parent in the use of the dictionary will ensure that it gets used at home as well as school. However, no definitions are provided: it is specifically a spelling dictionary.

*Word Bank* from Collins Educational is an excellent basic spelling dictionary with a thesaurus function. It is very accessible, as you can judge for yourself by looking at sample pages on the Collins website: www.collinseducation.com

Dictionary practice may be an old-fashioned concept, but it is still a very useful activity, and can be great fun if done against a timer for a lesson 'starter' or 'finisher' lasting only a few minutes. The activity can be styled a 'dictionary derby', and pupils can be allowed to work in pairs to take off the pressure. Appendix 4.7 describes another lively spelling game, based on *Who Wants to be a Millionaire*.

### Reinforcing key words

It is pleasing that more and more classrooms have displays of key words on the wall. I would, however, counsel that plenty of space is used around the words and that the difficult sections are highlighted in the manner outlined above. The words also need to be fairly large or they simply will not be noticed!

We are, of course, also catering for the students who have visual difficulties as well as those students who should be wearing their glasses and don't! If we really want the words to be noticed, why not hang them from the ceiling so that they rotate like a mobile? This gives out the message that key words are a central, not a peripheral, part of learning, as well as making them easier to see.

## Supporting students with scotopic sensivity

Daryl was a real nuisance in the classroom – a real cat on hot bricks – often defacing or screwing up worksheets placed in front of him. When we eventually had a civil conversation about these incidents he admitted that the paper seemed to 'glare' at him. We tried some different coloured overlays. He found that pale blue seemed to help and 'calm down the paper'. It seems to have calmed him down quite a bit too, though not completely!

You may have some students who have scotopic sensitivity (or Irlen Syndrome) and others who have it and do not realise it. Try to use a colour other than white as a background for worksheets *and* displays. If you highlight students' names in the relevant colour in your mark book, it will jog your memory when you need to reproduce worksheets for that group.

In any case, a display is likely to look more attractive in different colours. Most people who suffer from scotopic sensitivity use yellow backgrounds, but for some, other colours are more helpful. (Your SENCO will be able to tell you which colour a student needing this support is using.) If you use different coloured backgrounds in your display, you might discover a hidden sufferer who will tell you that he or she finds that mauve backgrounds, for example, are easier to read than anything else.

## Using computers to support writing

Students can take charge of their ongoing spelling needs by using the Autocorrect facility. They will find a number of words already there – but they can add their own in consultation with their teacher or TA. For example, they could enter 'gov' for 'government' and/or shd for 'should'. This will free them from the burden of trying to get everything right and should speed up the process of writing considerably.

> Terry was very resistant to writing when he first came to the school and had a very low level of self-esteem. What writing he did do was very messy and seemed to demonstrate a complete lack of care and interest. He was also disinclined to contribute orally, except to make interesting whooping noises which he would alternate with a deep growl for the sake of variety.
>
> We tried him with an Alphasmart word processor and it completely transformed his approach to his work. It seemed to confer dignity on him and as he said to us: 'It's as if my mistakes don't matter so much any more'. We also found that the need to download his work onto a PC for the sake of fine tuning and printing gave him a chance to demonstrate the sense of responsibility we knew he had from the stories we knew of him organising a stall at the school fete. He didn't have a computer at home and we felt able to trust him to take his Alpasmart home. His oral contributions have improved as well!
> (See: www.alphasmart.co.uk)

There are many students, and not just those with SEN, who avoid the challenge of using more complex vocabulary because they know they cannot spell the words they want. Teachers may be surprised about how far up the scale of importance it is for many students. We should not underestimate the desire of all students to get the spelling right!

James set very high standards for himself. His oral contributions were very good; his written output was usually brief and unfinished. He always wanted to experiment with new vocabulary but was hamstrung by his inability to spell the words he wanted. He has been taught to use the thesaurus function to good effect.

He now feels able to use complicated words in his writing by calling up the thesaurus, typing in a straightforward word that means the same, and then looking at the alternatives suggested. He can usually recognise the one he wants. For example, if he wanted 'facilitate' he might type in 'help'.

More sophisticated programs which can be of terrific benefit to dyslexics and others are predictive word-processor packages such as *Read and Write* from textHELP and *Write Out Loud!* from Don Johnston Special Needs software suppliers. Crick software also market a system called *Penfriend*. These programs have the benefit of learning individual styles of spelling and writing and predicting what the student is going to write next. The students can then hear the text read back to them. The sophistication of these products means that able dyslexics in the sixth form can also benefit. They are also a fantastic resource for an increasing number of students who are being labelled 'mildly dyslexic'. You could seek to make your whole school 'dyslexia friendly' by buying a site licence – although this would require a financial and training commitment from your senior management.

Carla is a very high-achieving student. She has to do a lot of written work, but has been hampered by a significant degree of dyslexia. For most writing she uses a portable computer, but mostly she prefers to write the first draft by herself using the predictive word function alongside her word processor.

When she is unsure how to spell a word, she can type in the first letter and the program will provide a list of possible words which make sense in the context of the sentence she is writing. The list of words will appear in a dark blue box, preceded by a number. She can choose the right word, type in its number, and it will appear in her sentence. If she is still unsure, she can type the next letter and the list will change to show further likely alternatives.

The program has a dictionary of around 10,000 words. It is also able to remember which words she uses most often and these will come up first. Additional words can be added to the dictionary by the user. Carla feels completely liberated by the facility.

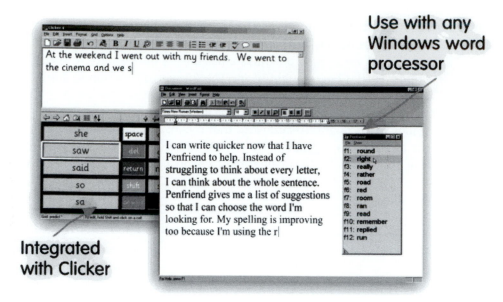

**Use with any Windows word processor**

At the weekend I went out with my friends. We went to the cinema and we s|

**Integrated with Clicker**

I can write quicker now that I have Penfriend to help. Instead of struggling to think about every letter, I can think about the whole sentence. Penfriend gives me a list of suggestions so that I can choose the word I'm looking for. My spelling is improving too because I'm using the r|

**Figure 4.8** *Penfriend*

## Building sentences

Effective writing is, of course, about far more than just effective spelling. Weaker students often struggle to understand the patterns of words – the grammatical structures which have been unconsciously internalised by more confident writers.

Many English teachers will be familiar with Andrew Moore's excellent website of free resources: www.shunsley.eril.net/armoore/default.htm. It is well worth regular visits! He suggests the use of colour coding to highlight different categories of words. On the next page is his advice for building and understanding the nature of sentences.

Any student can have enormous fun with this. It would obviously be a good idea for at least a whole-department agreement on colour coding. It would be beneficial for SEN students for the most important parts of speech to be coded in bright primary colours. This would also aid the student with a degree of colour-blindness.

In marking work, the teacher could choose for one week to emphasise the adjectives in a piece of work. The following week it could be nouns, and so on.

Colour is easy to apply to text. It is usual to find it on the right-hand side of the second toolbar (the one with **B** *I* <u>U</u> on it). On later versions of Word you may have to click on a double arrowhead (>>) at the edge of this toolbar to reveal it.

## Improving keyboarding skills

One way of improving keyboarding skills this is to run a Keyboard Club, perhaps in the lunch hour, when the students can come in and use specific typing programs. We should not be aiming to create brilliant touch typists but to

Write a model sentence, and then ask the students to replace any words with other words of the same grammatical category. For example, start with this sentence:

The witty young teacher thoughtfully wrote a silly sentence.

Then replace the coloured words with other words of the same colour (and category) from the table below:

| ADJECTIVE | NOUN | ADVERB | TRANSITIVE VERB |
|---|---|---|---|
| big, little, happy, friendly, sad, unusual, ridiculous, blue, intelligent | octopus, fish, anteater, teapot, motorbike, banana, football, roundabout, xylophone, fieldmouse, toilet, boy, girl, man, woman | happily, rapidly, slowly, carefully, wisely, regularly, confidently, patiently, gently | bit, kissed, touched, ate, cuddled, fondled, rode, struck, tortured |

With luck you will get a surreal but grammatically sound sentence like:

The toxic pink aardvark patiently fondled a drunken lifeboat.

The ridiculous pink fish carefully rode a little bicycle.

Pupils may illustrate these while labelling and colouring the word categories/parts of speech!

*Figure 4.9*

increase pupils' familiarity with the qwerty keyboard. Using a keyboard program such as *Type to Learn* will facilitate this. The aim should be the creation of typists who can type at least as fast as they would otherwise write. I speak as an unrepentant two-finger typist who can do this simply as a result of years of experience tapping away. This is an important point because you will encounter students who will be reluctant to use the computer because they cannot find the appropriate keys fast enough. It can be soul-destroying for a pupil who struggles with writing to find that using a computer takes even longer.

## Responding to writing

Encourage students to double space their writing. This will make it much easier for them to work on redrafting and proof-reading and is good advice for students of all abilities. It also makes it easier for the teacher to give clear feedback to a first draft.

Weaker students can find the process of redrafting and proof-reading threatening since it is likely to reveal more than the usual number of errors in their writing. Avoid falling into the trap of correcting everything. Help them to identify patterns of errors which may occur several times in a piece of writing, for example changing 'y' to 'ies' in plural words, or misusing singular and plural verbs. If we wish them to write, we need to build up their confidence. It goes without saying that we should find something to praise in every piece of work, and that 'praise' comments should always outnumber 'negatives'.

### Using Crick Computer Software Support for Writing

*The Assassin* exercise (Appendix 4.10) would lend itself very easily to being presented in *Wordbar* (Crick software). *Wordbar* is an incredibly powerful program with enormous potential for the English department. It is a toolbar that sits along the bottom of the computer screen. The student can click on words and phrases in *Wordbar* to send them to any word processor. It has:

- rapid point-and-click access to thousands of words

- reputedly, the latest speech technology

Words and phrases in *Wordbar* are organised into tabs and the user just clicks on to a tab to see a different set of words. It comes with high-quality software speech so the students can hear words or phrases before they write them. Simplified instructions for starting *Wordbar* can be found in Appendix 4.8.

Here are just a very few examples of the massive number of grids that are available:

- adjectives which may be used in writing about people, grouped under characteristics such as height, build and mood;

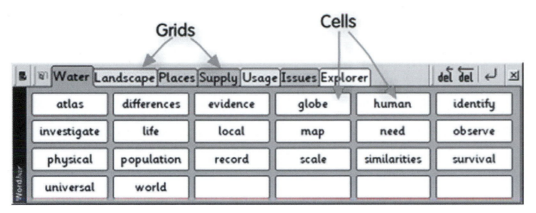

**Figure 4.10** *Wordbar*

- wordlists to support writing about five particular settings – a beach, a castle, a city, a forest and a garden – each of which has two word banks, nouns and descriptors;

- vocabulary to support written work about the main characters in *Great Expectations*;

- vocabulary to support *sequencing* in *Great Expectations*;

- general vocabulary for writing about Shakespeare's plays;

- a list of useful terms for a piece of writing about how language is used in a text.

Again, investment in a networked program could be of enormous benefit.

> Dinesh responds well to ICT and is very confident in front of a computer, in marked contrast to the plain white page. He loves reading and literature but is highly frustrated by the slow process of recording his thoughts. He has very serious handwriting problems, largely due to his dyspraxia. Having recourse to the words and phrases of *Wordbar* reduces the effort needed on the keyboard. He can still edit the phrases if they don't quite do justice to his thoughts. Dinesh backs this up with keyboard practice in lunchtime sessions. In this way he can feel liberated from his recording difficulties while separately developing his keyboard skills.

*Wordbar* is available from Crick software. There is an excellent Powerpoint presentation on the Crick website (www.cricksoft.com) about the features of *Wordbar* which is worth downloading to help convince sceptical colleagues that it is worth using on a school-wide, or at least department-wide, scale.

A newer program from Crick software with just as much potential is *Cloze-Pro*:

- The student simply clicks on letters, words or phrases in the grid to fill the highlighted gap in the text.

- Activities are easy to set up – the teacher has just to copy and paste text into *ClozePro* and then take out every seventh word, or specify the number of words to remove.

- It can provide structured reports for you to track a child's progress in the activities, including information on the prompts used and the attempts made.

- It has high-quality software speech so children can hear the words in the grid, or the activity text, before they answer.

- *ClozePro* comes with a Picture Library to illustrate the activities. You can also use your own pictures.

- There is a wide range of accessibility options for people who cannot use a mouse or keyboard. The company can also provide a wide range of access devices.

- The teacher can choose which words to remove depending on the learning task. Words can be deleted according to specific criteria, e.g. adjectives, conjunctions or facts. So students:

  - can show knowledge of a subject;

  - can check their own knowledge of a subject;

  - can practise using particular language;

  - can be encouraged to consider the effectiveness of a particular word within a sentence;

  - can practise a skill taught in a lesson, e.g. using past/present verb tenses;

  - can be encouraged to use the context of a passage, e.g. they can find the correct word by reading further on.

*ClozePro* features that encourage or help students to work independently are:

- *Speech* – the students can listen to the passage and the missing words;

- *Prompts* – the teacher can set up different prompts depending on the ability of the student;

- *Different gap styles* – these give clues to students and the style of the gaps for the same exercise can be changed according to each student's ability, for differentiation (equal length gaps for all words, gaps that show the word length, asterisks to show the number of letters, blurred gaps to show the shape of the words, or less blurred gaps for a word-matching exercise);

- *Changing the number of missing words displayed* – you can limit the number of words for students who need more help and display more words for other students, but use the same exercise, for differentiation.

You can print out worksheets for follow-up activities, or to have activities without the support features mentioned above, or for homework.

## Do you have enough access to computers?

A critical matter, of course, is access to computers. Many schools are better resourced than they used to be in this area. However, if your school does not fall into this category, you may wish to use some of the ideas suggested in this book to convince your head teacher of the benefits of investing in computers to support your English teaching across the ability range. You do not need the most up-to-date computers to use the basic functions of Microsoft Word in the ways I have suggested. Local businesses who are upgrading their systems might be willing to donate some of their older machines to your department.

When I last looked, there were refurbished laptop computers with a 500 mhz processor available for around £410 including VAT. You would obviously have to consult your own ICT department for their views on this.

An alternative approach is to buy new but very basic word processors as supplied by companies such as ianSYST or TAG Developments. These have limited functions although they do include a spell-checker and a grammar check. The latest ones often have a predictive word function which is both fun and enormously liberating. They can also download easily onto a PC using a supplied cable or an infrared port (a little more expensive). They cost from between £150 and £300. If money is tight, try and do a joint deal with your SEN department.

> Lauren does not have access to a computer at home so she is loaned an Alphasmart for use at home. However, she finds she can manage her homework better if she stays behind after school and works in the Learning Support Room with a group of students. She is using a desktop word processor, and has a small portable computer on the desk beside her which she has learnt to download into the PC.

*AlphaSmart 2000* and *Type to Learn* are available from TAG Developments and also from ianSYST.

## Low-tech equipment

Pupils with SEN frequently come to lessons poorly equipped. If you have a dyslexic and/or dyspraxic student in your classroom with their equipment it will almost certainly be accidental as they often have poorly developed organisational skills. As teachers, we may feel that the least a child can do is to come to school with the basic equipment. However, we may be judging them by our own standards. For a variety of reasons, this may not be a priority in their world. We are dealing with children who are unlikely to spend their Saturday mornings pouring over the pen counter at W. H. Smith's.

The following suggestions might help:

- Don't make the lack of equipment a battleground area.

- Keep a stationery box in your classroom containing a range of pens, including Berol handwriters, needlepoint pens, roller balls, plastic nibbed fountain pens, and the new Staedler curvy topped pen. You could use a loan system to ensure their return. Avoid the temptation to buy cheap biros which use cheap, thick, sticky ink which is difficult to control and has a tendency to blot and smudge.

- Offer positive rewards if pupils remember their own equipment, a loan pen if they don't.

- You could operate a purchasing scheme in partnership with a local supplier. I have found that carefully selected SEN students can make excellent custodians of the stock. I know of one school where the librarian runs a basic stationery shop in the library and another where it is organised by the parent/teacher association.

For a low-tech vocabulary-building game, see Appendix 4.9.

## Handwriting

Students will enjoy experimenting with different pens and this is also a good strategy to try before you refer a poor handwriter to the SEN department.

Here are some more suggestions:

- Once the student has decided on their ideal pen and they have bought their own, remembering equipment could be a class/subject target for them.

- Use peer mentoring. Jenny could help Jimmy with his handwriting by providing a role model for him. We need to empower Jimmy in this regard. His target could be to look at two or three of his worst letters and decide to concentrate on those for a week. If he has chosen Jenny as his mentor he will have looked at the way she has formed the letters which cause him the most problems and will attempt to copy her style for a week. Jenny will gently remind him about his targets each English lesson because handwriting habits, like all bad habits, can be very hard to break.

- Set individual targets to work on within the context of the classroom. We could give Jimmy a hundred handwriting worksheets to do outside the classroom and he could fill them in superbly. In my experience, however, the lessons learned in this manner rarely transfer to the classroom.

## The P, E and S stages of assessing handwriting

Turner and Pughe describe this model in their book, *English and Dyslexia*. It is well worth consulting as it is packed with excellent advice.

*The P stage* deals with *posture, pen grip* and *paper position*:

- *Posture* – Is Jimmy slouched over the table or sitting in an upright but relaxed position? Is the chair the right height for the desk?

- *Pen grip* – Is Jimmy holding the pen about 2 cm from the pen point? Does he use a tense, awkward grip? If he does, this can be a very difficult habit to break at secondary level. A sloping board might be a worth a try (old-fashioned school desks had this slope built in!)

- *Paper position* – Right-handers should have the paper slanted slightly to the left and vice versa for left-handers. The other hand should act as a balance.

## The E (Essential) stage

First targets should be considered at this stage:

- Turner and Pughe feel strongly that there should be short-term targets which address a cursive script for students who print. I feel that in this case it might be more appropriate to target two to three letters to join up. Perhaps I think this because my own handwriting is so poor and I have adopted this target for myself!

- Writing on the line could be a very appropriate first target for some students. Just on its own it can make a real difference to presentation.

## The S (Specific) stage

At this stage, attention should be paid to the following points:

- The student needs to decide which way his letters are going to slant, and keep it that way.

- The student should aim to make small letters roughly half the size of the ascenders and descenders and of the same size.

- Turner and Pughe recommend the use of special writing paper which has small blue lines in between the middle lines for guidance purposes.

> The key to legibility for Errol is to 'unjoin' some of his letters. He chooses the selection that he is focusing on during that week at Monday registration. He agrees his selection with his mentor. He and his mentor then meet at Friday breaktime to decide how successfully the target has been met. If it has, Errol is praised. The following Monday, he chooses a new selection of letters. He may well then partially forget last week's target, but over the period of half a term he is absorbing the message to only join up on average three letters at a time.

The strategy described above would again seem to fly in the face of received wisdom, but a study of many neat handwriters in your classroom will show that they tend only to join up about three letters at a time.

Don't worry if your own handwriting leaves something to be desired in terms of attractiveness. If this is the case, Jimmy and Errol can more easily understand that *they* don't have to write neatly all the time provided, of course, that their writing is legible, if not beautiful. Rough notes in workbooks are acceptable as long as they can still read them the following lesson.

We are entering the realm of peer tutoring here. Tutoring pairs need to be chosen and monitored carefully to make sure that the arrangement is beneficial to both parties, and obviously not entered into if either side is at all reluctant. This operates most effectively when both tutor and 'tutee' understand their respective roles and the objectives of the exercise. Some training for tutors would be valuable, covering the following points:

- how to support rather than 'do it for them'

- how to build up self-esteem and confidence

- how to emphasise what is done 'right' or 'nearly right' rather than what is 'wrong'

It is best to concentrate on just one area. With Jimmy and Errol it is their handwriting. They may also have spelling problems but we should address them in a different way. Moderate spelling difficulties, for example, can be very usefully addressed by tutoring pairs, using the methods outlined above.

Any doubt on the mentor's part can be resolved by dictionary work (one assumes an English classroom has them readily to hand) and this is one example of how peer tutoring can be mutually beneficial. It is useful to have a mini-contract drawn up between the pair so that you have a built-in review time. There is evidence to suggest that these arrangements can have a quite dramatic short-term improvement, but they can be difficult to sustain unless fairly closely monitored.

## Other aspects of differentiation

Every teacher is familiar with the philosophy of differentiation, and everybody knows that it is often the most difficult thing to do well. It isn't always about having different work for different people. A substantial investment in ICT along the lines suggested above will address some of the issues, as well as some particular ICT programmes to be outlined below. The classic reluctant writer will need a good deal of support in developing his or her ideas.

See Appendices 4.10–4.15 for some ideas for 'scaffolding writing'. I have found that the effect of this 'scaffolding' is to give the writer confidence. They do not have to keep rigidly to this structure but they always have something to refer to when wondering what to write next – and the teacher or TA input can be minimal – the equivalent of a nudge in the right direction.

I have also found it to be enough to get some students away and writing just because they know they have something to which they can refer. Thus, I feel we are encouraging independence by giving them the freedom to depart from this structure if they wish, but they have a resource to fall back on which does not require them to be constantly asking 'What do I write next?'

It obviously pays to think of differentiation in a school-wide context rather than something that just applies to pupils with SEN. If your school has not already done so, some sort of screening to ascertain the preferred learning style of incoming students is important, just as much as ascertaining a profile of the intakes' reading and spelling ability. Are they primarily visual, auditory or kinaesthetic learners? Alastair Smith (1997) offers one method of finding this out. Walker (2002) lists, for example, twenty-five strategies for kinaesthetic learners which include:

- role play

- underlining /highlighting key words

- making a leaning map

- demonstrating a concept as if to a deaf person

- applying actions to words and phrases

Smith gives further guidance on what visual learners require:

- visual display opportunities above eye level in the room (many secondary classrooms do not maximise the opportunities)

- video, OHP, coloured board markers

- key words displayed around the room

Auditory learners need:

- paired and group discussions

- mini-debates

- tape, sound bites

- raps, rhyme, chants and verse, dramatic readings

- mnemonics

## Clearly defined structure to lessons

A clearly defined structure is something that all students need – no teacher would seriously argue that it was unimportant except in very special circumstances. However, there are elements which are particularly important for students with special needs.

The model advocated by the Literacy Progress Units, outlined below, is worth trying on a larger scale. It seems to work for me!

---

**Objectives:** Make it clear what the students should achieve by the end of the session.

**Remember to establish the context:** Students need to get a sense of the 'big picture' – where the subject fits in their understanding; work from previous sessions is *briefly reviewed.*

**Model:** Demonstrate what you want the students to do. Explain *how* you did what you did! New information presented in a variety of ways: visual, auditory, kinaesthetic.

**Try** pupils' own version – you will have writing frames and ICT hardware and software to support this process. If it is an oral activity, let them try paired work and then perhaps expand into small-group work. Students experiment with and test their understanding with each other and with you.

**Apply** what students have learnt to a new context with the same level of support. Allow lots of thinking time backed up with prompt questions and further writing support if necessary.

**Secure** feedback from the students to check for understanding. Explain links from this lesson to the next lesson. Students will be encouraged to think about *how* they have learned.

---

*Figure 4.11* Model from Literacy Progress Units

## Homework

Always attempt to set homework halfway or three-quarters of the way through the lesson. If left to the end, students may find it difficult to concentrate on the details and end up writing down something which they will not be able to understand later. Consider photocopying the task and handing it out instead of expecting pupils to write it down. Some homework ideas are suggested in Appendix 4.16.

CHAPTER 5

# Monitoring and Assessment

Assessment should provide feedback on the progress pupils make, and identify which areas need to be improved and how the student can achieve this. It is important that teachers communicate judgements about achievement and effort to pupils in a way that they will understand and appreciate, rather than allowing students with SEN to become used to low scores and lots of red pen. The marking of spelling, in particular, needs a careful and consistent approach.

There are many schools where the IEP process is fully integrated within the assessment processes of the school, but equally there are others in which the SENCO is embroiled in mountains of paperwork and in churning out loads of IEPs which may have little relevance for the classroom teacher, or at any rate in setting targets which are difficult to achieve in the classroom. This problem has been exacerbated in recent years by database software that may be able to produce an IEP in twenty seconds, but it may be one that has little ownership from anybody, least of all for the student for whom it is designed.

## Targets

A further issue for English departments is that many targets/aims that are set may be interpreted as being directly relevant to English. Long-term aims, for example, may include the need to develop/extend/improve any of the following:

- understanding/use of language

- understanding of grammatical terms

- ability to follow increasingly difficult instructions

- speaking skills

- personal vocabulary

- social, interactional and co-operative skills

- literacy – confident use of high frequency words, awareness of essential phonics

- spelling, comprehension, free writing

- reading skills – greater fluency, more confident use of word-attack strategies

- more legible handwriting

- independent learning, e.g. confident use and organisation of low-vision aids to aid learning for a pupil with moderate visual impairment

- self-confidence, e.g. development of greater oral language skills to improve communication in the hearing world for a pupil with moderate or more severe hearing loss

- daily and longer term organisational skills

- completion of classwork, homework and meeting deadlines

- confident use of ICT for independent working

It is unlikely of course, that any one statement or IEP would identify all of these targets and, in any case, IEPs should nowadays have a maximum of three to four SMART targets (Specific, Measurable, Achievable, Relevant, Timed) rather than vague and long-term aims such as to 'improve reading'. In many cases, the SENCO ends up doing all the SEN paperwork without any useful input from colleagues, and this makes it difficult for IEPs to be an integral part of the assessment procedure of the school, as they should be.

We need to ensure that the student is interested in improving. We cannot do that if we do not, first of all, praise and recognise effort made, which of course should be judged against the standards set by the students themselves. The new Code of Practice for SEN is moving to a model which puts the student at the centre of the process. Setting targets is something that is done *with* the students and not *to* them.

This works at several levels: students need to share or participate in setting the assessment objectives; they need to be involved in the assessing of work either through self or peer assessment; and they need to consider how to use the information to improve their work in future. (See Appendix 5.1 for a sample of a self-evaluation sheet.) The Ofsted document *Good Assessment Practice in English* (HMI 1473 2003) provides much thought-provoking advice about assessment in English. It makes the following observations about effective practice:

- Targets are subject-specific, of manageable proportions (e.g. the spelling of a number of key words, the reading of a particular book), achievable and observable.

- Targets are relatively short-term and subject to regular amendment.

- Targets are stored in a place where they are accessible to the pupil as they undertake the next task (e.g. a planner or draft book).

- Targets are drawn from, or relate to, the teaching objectives of a unit of work or the assessment criteria for the current task, and so are immediately relevant and can be referred to in marking and feedback.

- Pupils do not have too many simultaneous targets in English or school-wide.

- Targets are derived from teachers' assessments and are not only pupil-devised.

The document is, of course, referring to target setting for all students and not just those with SEN. It states further that:

> . . . the most important feature of the best practice in English assessment is the detailed knowledge good specialist teachers have of their pupils as learners. This is reflected in and dependent on careful, targeted questioning to check understanding and detailed marking of written work with suggestions for improvement.

## IEPs

A key phrase in the new SEN Code of Practice is that IEPs should identify provision and procedures that are 'additional to' and 'different from' those which are normally available to all students. These key phrases are designed to help schools cut down on the amount of paperwork they are required to do. This should free them up to put more of their effort into planning, implementing and evaluating provision rather than into generating large numbers of IEPs. It does, however, place an onus on the school to provide effective approaches to differentiation, so that the majority of needs are met by good classroom practice and a common desire to overcome barriers to learning.

While targets are written for and applied to the individual student, the classroom approach to specific types of targets may well be general. It is unlikely, for example, that you will encounter only one student for whom effective listening is an issue, or that the target set for one 'listening deficient' student is fundamentally different from that needed by another.

If your school's IEPs are not very user-friendly, it might be an opportunity for a joint English department/SEN initiative to render them useable at classroom level. Alternatively, you might find that your SEN department would welcome the opportunity to completely overhaul the systems and would value an ally, as more and more SEN departments are trying to rationalise the paperwork burden and only produce material that is of positive use. This might be particularly important if you as a department feel that IEPs are a 'bolt-on' feature of your school. For example, if the IEP specifically states as a target that the second hundred most common words are to be checked for accuracy, it is vital to establish who should be assessing what at review time. Does the SENCO expect you to know what the 'second hundred' words are? Even if the SENCO does not expect you to monitor this target, you need to know the classroom implications for a student for whom the second hundred most common words in the English language are a major problem. One obvious implication, for example, is that the child will be severely limited in the area of creative writing.

A problem for some schools is access to the detail of these IEPs – not just for the teachers but for the students themselves. Some schools, and indeed individual departments, use a simple chart to specify individual targets. This chart is stuck on the inside cover of exercise books or homework planners (in the case of school-wide targets). This keeps them accessible and in the forefront of the student's and teacher's mind. Quite clearly, this could be a strategy which could and should work for all students and not just those with SEN. The targets could be negotiated once a term. One target could be literacy based, one behaviour, and one 'English specific', e.g:

1. I will always read through my work and ask a friend to read it to make sure it makes sense.

2. I will try to answer at least one question in every lesson.

3. I will ask myself 'why?' when I write down an answer in order to check whether I can write more.

The HMI document, *Good Assessment Practice in English*, would seem to endorse this idea:

> Practice is most effective where the assignment objectives are clearly displayed (for example on a cover sheet specific to the task) or pupils are used to working as 'response partners', with a clear agenda of points to cover in looking at each others' work . . . The best departments use self- and peer-assessment to increase awareness of the nature of progress rather than seeing it as part of assessment itself – the latter being the preserve of the skilled, specialist English teacher.

In my own school, peer marking is gaining momentum. To quote the teachers' views:

> Lots of people are beginning to experiment with this process. It helps students to become familiar with exam board criteria, it can serve to raise self-esteem, and it offers other models for students to try out for themselves. Most people felt this was an area for development and believed that it would lead to improved student performance.

The same group felt very strongly about feedback:

> Both written comments and peer assessment are helpful, but nothing can beat one to one discussion. This does mean a restructuring of lesson time, to allow proper, meaningful feedback. It may mean that you cannot feedback to everyone on the same day. But, there was a strong sense in which people thought this would make students feel valued and may help them to progress.

Obviously here we have a situation where English staff are making time and space for target-setting and review to take place within the context of the lesson and also, by implication, setting a timescale for that review.

The HMI document warns English departments to ensure that the curriculum:

. . . offers pupils the greatest possible opportunity to demonstrate their learning, so that those who are more visual can produce texts using the media or ICT, those who best show their insight through role play and drama have a chance to do so, while those for whom a critical essay or a poem are the best medium to express their ideas can regularly produce these.

The document further cites an example where the school had carefully provided the appropriate task to match the attainment of the students:

. . . the Year 7 pupils were all working on fiction of the supernatural (or 'imagined worlds') but groups based on reading assessments were formed to match texts and tasks for each group to their level of attainment and reading targets.

Jean Gross argued in the autumn 2003 edition of the magazine *Special* that measurable, but highly generalised, targets could achieve the following:

- increase the percentage of children who, having started their key stage with below average attainment, have by the end of that key stage made progress at above the average national rate;

- reduce the frequency with which pupils are sent out of lessons to 'timeout' /withdrawal rooms;

- increase the frequency of the social integration of pupils with severe or complex SEN as measured by the amount of time they spend interacting with others in the playground.

Gross goes further to say that:

The difference between targets of this kind and IEP targets is that they are based in whole school measures rather than on individual children. They allow the school to challenge and evaluate itself in relation to outcomes for their provision as a whole . . .

The article quotes Kingsbridge Community College in Devon who have written IEPs for only the most needy students (the twenty or so who are on statements). Instead of IEPs, they have:

- a 'Watch-out' list for students who would have been on School Action and presumably School Action Plus, and around fifty students for whom classroom teachers need further information.

- 'Student Information Sheet' which gives bullet points detailing the specific concerns and suggested action points for staff to consider taking. The bottom half of the sheet is left for teachers to keep working notes under two headings – 'Problems relevant to this subject' and 'Action taken to ensure success in this subject'.

With suitable approaches to differentiation in place, the teaching staff should be able to enact an agreed and appropriate response.

## IEP layout and format

There are many and varied layouts for IEPs. Your school may be following your particular county line but there is no legal obligation to do so – provided of course that the proforma adopted satisfies their criteria. I particularly like Shropshire County Council's version (examples given in Appendix 5.2), as all the vital information that you need is provided on one sheet. It gives a succinct pen portrait detailing strengths first (most important), areas to be developed, and how the targets are going to be met, as well as identifying the role of everybody connected with the student concerned. The student's own role is, of course, clearly identified as well.

## Exams and assessment

Students have traditionally been assessed in numerical terms (7/10) or perhaps more commonly in English, in terms of A, B or C. It is, perhaps, human nature to look at the grade rather than the comments that should provide pointers to improvement.

One Head of English in Cumbria developed a sensitive method of grading work according to a student's individual standards. Consequently, rather than letters or numbers, he favoured the following symbols with their relevant meanings:

= this work is of your normal, expected standard

+ significantly better than your normal standard

++ excellent – amongst your best work this year

– not up to your usual standard

– – very disappointing. What went wrong?

Of course, the normal expected standard (=) would need to be reviewed on an annual or termly basis.

One English department that switched abruptly from A–D grades based on standards compared within the group, to NC descriptors based on levels, and in KS4 to grades A–G based on what that piece of work was worth in GCSE terms. Students who were getting F and G grades could not see their work in any other terms than it being rubbish as it seemed to be so far removed from grades A and B. The department felt that they had explained the rationale to the students (it had taken five minutes at the beginning of one lesson and a rather terse letter home) but had failed. It was, of course, due to the national obsession with levels A–C as being the 'good' GCSEs. By definition, the rest must be 'bad' GCSEs. The whole school, never mind the English department, must be sure that they explicitly value the D–G grades and take the trouble to identify career pathways that are open to D–G students. This can avoid the tiresome refrain from those students who state that there is little point in doing the work as the exam is worthless anyway.

## Liaison with further education

Liaison with local further education colleges and indeed local major employers would help to 'dignify' these grades. This becomes even more important if you are actively using Entry Level Certificate exams. I have found that both employers and further education staff are often very happy to contribute in a very practical way to this process by helping to assess the oral component of Entry level courses. Where this takes the form of a mock interview it is particularly effective! It is a matter of some debate whether or not the nature of Key Stage 4 English schemes of work at GCSE have become progressively less accessible to the less able.

## Objective measures of ability

What is vital is that English departments have some objective measure to place alongside their subjective judgements about who is suitable for what type of course. NFER tests such as the Cognitive Ability Test can provide an exceptionally detailed profile of each learner's potential (at a price) at Key Stage 3 and at GCSE. NFER also separately publish detailed advice on how to interpret scores. (There would obviously have to be a whole-school commitment to introducing such a test on grounds of cost.) There are other tests which can give a similar, if less detailed and reliable indicator, such as the NFER group reading test. This is a test that measures reading comprehension rather than just word-attack skills. The former usually, but not always, scores lower and provides a reasonable indication of ability.

Students scoring around 70 in Year 7 are likely to be severely challenged by GCSE English. Students scoring less than 80 on this test should have their progress closely monitored. One option that many departments take is for a number of students to follow both GCSE and Entry level courses for a while, and the ultimate decision about which exam to enter is deferred to a particular date. One way of making this approach effective is to work thematically on the original writing and speaking and listening course components. If these are attempted at the start of Year 10, students transferring to Entry level can still make use of the work undertaken.

It is obviously vital that other, more subjective, factors are taken into account when forming a picture of a student. Do they have a phobia about examinations, for example?

## Ways of testing

Ask yourself *why* you are testing before you actually do so. Is the manner in which you are testing bound to result in wholly predictable scores (Jenny Sweetipie always gets 90% and Jimmy Clueless inevitably gets 10%)? or, can you devise a way to enable all pupils to show what they do know and *have* learned? The best sort of test actually helps to cement knowledge and can even be fun! Here are some suggestions:

- You could have a series of statements and the students have to decide whether they are true or false. You could add a further criteria 'not enough evidence' which is a technique used by the Oxford University Press in their *Headwork* books.

- Match questions to answers or words to definitions. If this is networked on computer, the students could drag and drop the phrases in order to achieve the right pairings.

- The Crick software program *ClozePro* described in Chapter 4 has obvious potential for testing purposes.

- You could give parts of the test to your ADHD students in more than one sitting – because you are testing knowledge and not attention span.

- Students need to be familiar with the format of the exams as well as the nature of the questions. The game format (e.g. Word Dominoes) could be used to help students with the meaning of exam terminology.

- Supply key words for the particular subject under examination and get the class or pairs of students to decide how they link. Powell describes this as a 'word-train'. For example, words like 'anger-violence-death-escape-love-marriage' could be linked thus when considering the themes of *Romeo and Juliet.*

- Another Powell (1997) idea is 'Matchmakers' where students have cards with a question, and an answer relating to a different question on it. Students in the class have to call out the question on their card and the others have to see whether the answer on their card matches it.

- An excellent Cutting Edge idea is *Word Dominoes.* A card 'domino' with Love/Poison on it, for example, can be linked to another with Death/Humour on it, and so on.

## Special exam considerations

There is a wide range of dispensations available for exams at both Key Stage 3 and 4. The choice is limited for English students and this is something which SENCOs have long found frustrating. Examination boards hold that one of the things that they are examining is the ability to write coherently. This ignores the plight of the able dyslexic who may be able to analyse literature and language brilliantly in an oral manner but cannot convey those same ideas in written form.

It is worth making friends with the educational psychologist serving your school. Too often the only teachers s/he comes into contact with are the SEN staff.

The English teacher can ask for:

- *Additional time* – boards have little problem in granting 25% extra time but you may have some significantly dyslexic students who could benefit from more time than this – this would have to be negotiated with the SENCO and the board. You need to consider carefully whether this is appropriate for some students who might be better served by having a chance to retake a test or to take it at a different time of day.

- *Breaks between questions* – this will sometimes be granted in addition to the above. It is a good strategy for dyspraxic students who do not feel sufficiently confident with word-processing or for any student who has significant difficulties controlling a pen. Writing uninterrupted for up to three hours can be an considerable strain. Check also that students are using a pen that is best suited to their needs. You may think you have got this aspect sorted out, but the dypraxic's tendency to disorganisation could mean that they have the wrong pen on the crucial day!

- *Use of a word processor* – this is useful for students who are confident in this medium and who have been using it as a normal strategy in the classroom. In other words, you cannot suddenly adopt this strategy with two weeks to go to the examination! Accept typed or word-processed assignments from likely students in good time. Exam centres have to be sure that the spell-checker facility has been disabled. Not all ICT staff seem to be able to do this. Check in good time that it really has been disabled! It can be something that an exam board spot check might want to verify.

- *Modified papers for those with poor sight* – visual impairments – exam boards can provide enlarged papers given sufficient notice. There is a deadline for notification.

- *Working alone* – this is expensive on supervision time but could make all the difference to the student with ADHD who might find the exam hall situation too distracting. The nightmare scenario for this student would be to attempt to distract another student – not only ruining his/her own chances but those of someone else as well.

- *Quiet room* – for school and/or examination phobics. Schools should take exam hall phobia seriously and treat it as a genuine special need. A student at my last school who was later to be diagnosed as agoraphobic attained a string of A and B grades having been granted this facility. Another school resisted making special arrangements for a pupil with Tourette's Syndrome until, by Year 10, he was uncontrollable and had to be given access to a quiet room for the sake of other students as well as himself. The improvement in his grades was nothing short of remarkable. The moral of this tale is 'don't delay'!

Whatever dispensations are granted, it is important that the individual students are able to practise them if they are to be ultimately helpful.

Not all pupils with SEN will 'qualify' for special arrangements but for those with significant special needs, they can make a big difference. There are strict timescales to be adhered to when applying for dispensations, and staff should refer to the annually updated regulations sent to all schools. Information about Key Stage 3 reporting and SAT arrangements is available on the QCA website: www.qca.org.uk/ages3–14/tests_tasks/

## Entry level or GCSE?

Entry level is an exam system designed to be the first level of the National Qualifications Framework that is aimed at students working at National Curriculum levels 1, 2 and 3. It is divided into three levels: 1, 2 and 3, with 3 being the highest and known as a distinction pass. There is some debate going on at present in order to achieve some sort of comparability between the highest level of Entry level and the lower levels of GCSE. Many English teachers believe very strongly that students who achieve distinction on Entry level are out-performing their peers at grade G and F of GCSE, and possibly even at grade E.

English certificates are made up of a number of units. Each unit is assessed separately so that each step of achievement may be recognised along the way to completing the full certificate.

There are a minimum number of units that must be included in a certificate but the choice of which ones can be left to the centre. This means that exam centres can match their course to the needs of their students.

Despite being aimed at levels 1–3 of the National Curriculum, other, more able, students may benefit from completing an Entry Level Certificate if they have behavioural difficulties which prevent them for one reason of another from attending school regularly. Other students might be in the following situations:

- pupil referral units (14- to 16-year-olds)
- further education colleges (16- to 19-year-olds)
- young offenders' institutions
- prison
- adult literacy classes – students who may have been out of the system for some time

There is tremendous flexibility with regard to timescale, although obviously schools would seek to complete the course within the two-year span of Key Stage 4, but this does, however, allow students who might seek to stay on for an additional year to continue working towards their Certificate or indeed continue with their work in a college of further education.

Students within a single group may make widely varying degrees of progress so that the course may be completed at different times. If this is the case, then there may be grounds for 'transfer' to GCSE, especially as the work can be tailored to mirror GCSE.

### *Assessment of Entry level work*

At least 40% of the course is assessed 'externally' in a modular fashion and in a variety of ways:

- set and marked by the awarding body
- set by the awarding body, marked by the centre and moderated by the awarding body

- designed by the centre, validated before use by the awarding body, marked by the centre and moderated by the awarding body

Practical, written or oral tasks are the basis of the tests and assignments. In National Curriculum based certificates, at least 50% of the content is assessed externally. Students tend to like the external assessments as they give a sense of legitimacy to the process. The remainder of the certificate is assessed by the centre. Usually students will put together a file which demonstrates evidence of their achievement. The evidence can be in a variety of forms such as video, audio witness statements and photographs.

Schools may consider dual entry for GCSE English Language (F or G grade) and Entry level. Equally, students could follow a dual course with a final decision time when entries have to be made.

## English speaking board

Most students would agree that developing their oral skills is likely to be helpful in their future. Students who enter the ESB examinations have thorough preparation in the skills they need. There are junior and senior programmes from Entry level to level 3 of the National Curriculum framework. They centre on four assessment tasks which explore a range of skills. The English Speaking Board states:

> In each series there is a common core of presentation skills and interactive questions and discussion. The presentation focuses on knowledge and skills in differing contexts based on the candidate's own experience, vocational contexts and interests . . . Other tasks depending on syllabus and level, may include literary interpretation through reading and memorisation, telephone and interviewing skills, current affairs, debate, etc.

Great Cornard Upper School in Sudbury in Suffolk, amongst many others, use this examination extensively. Su English is the co-ordinator at the school and she has found that the preparation and examinations are useful yardstick for students' GCSE Speaking and Listening component. The students generally outperform their GCSE predicted or target grade. The school uses the exam in Year 10, for disaffected and underachieving pupils, and for students in Year 12 for communication skills.

This is what one student, Dale, had to say about the English Speaking Board:

> Without it I wouldn't have got the GCSE grades I got, or had the confidence to perform as I did in front of interview panels. It has helped me think on my feet and not be afraid to say what I want . . . at work and in the army, it's all about communicating with your voice.

## Using Teaching Assistants to help with coursework

Coursework completion can be the bane of many English teachers' lives and it can be a major problem, not least in an organisational sense, for students with SEN. Using the subject-support agreement to be found in chapter 6, teachers can inform TAs of precisely what is required from the students. This could be a useful context for support staff to take pupils out of class to work on coursework on a rota basis or according to need – particularly those pupils who are poorly organised or those who are otherwise reasonably able but disaffected.

# Managing Support

Throughout this book, the generic term of 'Teaching Assistant' has been used – abbreviated to TA for ease of writing – when referring to adults other than teachers in the classroom. There is a range of alternative names in use for these valuable individuals, sometimes indicating a different role or level of expertise (Learning Support Assistant, Classroom Assistant, Special Support Assistant, Pupil Assistant, Statement Support Assistant). They may be a full-time or a part-time member of staff, or employed by a local authority support service.

## Introduction

Teaching Assistants are now more prevalent than ever before. They often have a defined career structure and may be ex-teachers who do not want the pressure of classroom teaching or prospective teachers finding out whether this is the job for them. It is important to take their role seriously and give time to working out the best way to use them – they can be an incredibly valuable resource. Their role may be defined in a number of different ways but may broadly fit into the following categories:

- supporting individuals
- supporting certain groups
- supporting pupils generally
- supporting the teacher

The first thing you need to do is to find out how the SENCO prioritises support within the school and how you can influence the amount of support available in English lessons. Different schools have different ways of allocating time to departments, and it may often be the case that the department that uses them best may get more allocated time than others. With authorities moving towards devolved funding arrangements, there is no longer the same onus on

SENCOs to attach hours rigidly to particular students. Here are some of the ways TAs may be allocated to departments:

- a certain number of hours per subject area – to be shared out by the HoD

- departments have to 'bid' for TA time

- 'specialist' TAs for specific departments

- where SENCO allocates time, they may well be more generous with staff known to use TAs 'properly'

In any sort of 'bidding' system – a department will benefit from being able to show how it uses TAs effectively and values them appropriately.

## The nature of support

It pays off to make time to get to know your TAs. Some may well be suffering from a feeling of inferiority. When schools take the trouble to canvas opinions from TAs they often report that they feel they have something like servant status. They are obviously neither teachers nor students, and yet they may feel that both parties treat them as such. Your school may already have a means of negotiating working arrangements – but if you haven't, it might he useful to devise your own departmental one.

Having another adult in your classroom can be a fantastic resource or an irksome burden. In either case, it is essential to have systems which help both sides to liaise, plan, evaluate, review, develop and improve. Good TAs often develop excellent rapport with difficult students and can offer useful guidance on the best ways of managing them. Early consultations of this nature can be an important first step to making a TA feel valued. It is important to remember, however, that most TAs are paid by the hour and are not contracted for school holidays. Many indeed will be part-time workers. Take the trouble to find out who works when, as this might have bearing on which TA can be most useful in the department.

One, usually peripheral, reason why people choose to become TAs is that the hours are parent friendly: after-school meetings are not. One way to get round this problem might be for an English department to commit part of its INSET budget for meetings with TAs. This could obviously include training days on subjects which might be particularly relevant to a TA (e.g. investigating alternative accreditation at Key Stage 4 or effective use of DfES literacy catch-up units). If TAs are to be paid their hourly rate for attending, it will certainly make for value for money! Likewise, attendance at departmental meetings is likely to gain greater commitment if the TAs are paid and sufficient notice is given. Careful note of the relevance of the meeting to TAs is important (remember to allow them to go once you get to the item about oral mark schemes).

## Teamwork problems

Whilst many TA-teacher relationships are happy ones, problems may arise:

- TAs might have an overbearing presence which targeted students might shrink from;

- a dependency culture might grow up with students acquiring a 'learned helplessness';

- a TA might enjoy pupils depending on her (e.g. I'm the only one who really understands Jimmy Smith);

- rather than be seen to be 'lacking in know-how', a TA might seem over-confident and give pupils wrong information;

- you might also be frustrated by the TA who seems to spend a lot of time sitting in a desk beside Jimmy Smith listening attentively to you like an extra pupil.

It is no good just having a departmental moan about how useless Mrs Scroggins is. The most important thing any department can do is to emphasise teamwork between the teacher and TA, and also provide a reasonably formal setting for dialogue such as the subject-support agreement outlined below, because these problems have to be addressed in the interests of the children.

It is perhaps obvious to say that the first item for discussion should concern what the TA is doing right. The TA is then much more likely to be open to discussion about some more thorny issues. If a TA says that the reason for being welded to the side of Jimmy Smith is that his statement specifies this, it is reasonable to ask to have a look at the appropriate section after you have explained the problem you have with this, because at the very least the appropriate section may give you clues as to how best to work with the student.

Most authorities are trying to move away from issuing statements which specify the numbers of hours allocated to a particular student, but when they do, they often stipulate that the provision should be in the context of a small group.

Some of these problems may, of course, may be down to your organisation of the lesson. Are you doing too much talking or reading, and therefore not allowing much opportunity for input from the TA? It may be that you really need to do this on occasion, so you need to let the TA know in advance. Does she *have* to be there when you are doing this? Is there something more useful she could be doing for you or someone else such as preparing a cloze exercise, or doing a readability study of a text you are introducing the following week?

## Quick fixes

One quick and effective way of involving a TA with the minimum of preparation and making him or her feel valued is to acknowledge the main occupational hazard of the subject teacher – their very expertise:

- Ask your TA to act in a 'quality control' function by asking you the question that the class dare not or will not ask.

- The TA may be very well aware that a number of students are still not clear about where to place commas, for example, and are disinclined to admit this because they know that you have explained them carefully for the previous three lessons.

- The repetition will remind many students with SEN of their previous learning.

Appendix 6.1 describes a 'charter of services' and I hope this is useful in helping to define the different but overlapping roles of a sixth-former, TA, and support teacher, and might serve as a source of discussion at departmental meetings.

## The case for withdrawal?

Withdrawal is an issue that must be handled carefully. However tempting it might be to get rid of the five biggest troublemakers for a cosy session with the TA, ask yourself honestly why you are doing it. Such pupils may well be in need of support, but it is not fair to present a TA with a group of pupils with behaviour issues, unless, of course, the TA has an excellent rapport with them. You retain overall responsibility for the behaviour of the whole group, and sometimes the TA's perception of rapport might be interpreted as a licence to 'muck about' by the individuals involved.

On the other hand, withdrawal is a wonderful opportunity for TAs to fulfil obligations for small-group work which may be required by statements, and also to permit access to ICT, which is perhaps the biggest enabler of all. It is also an opportunity for the quiet and unassuming members of the group, who frequently get overlooked, to have some appropriately challenging 'quality time' with their TA. It is amazing how such students are able to survive in the classroom, often with a little (or a lot of) help from their friends, while understanding very little. Indeed, 'survival' is often the objective for these students.

Understanding is something that the quieter members of a group with SEN may have long given up on. In particular, withdrawal with a TA gives an opportunity for close monitoring and development of speaking and listening skills, an area in which this latter group is often particularly poor. This may again be a focus for discussion with your TA.

## Managing the issue of confidentiality

It is axiomatic to state that managing confidentiality is vital – yet there may well be a tension between this and the justified desire of all departments within the school to have as much information about students as possible. Perhaps more than any other, English departments need to have detailed knowledge of literacy levels, particularly of pupils who demonstrate a mis-match between their writing and reading abilities and their speaking and listening abilities. It is absolutely vital that you have this information from the first day the students enter the school, to avoid highly damaging comments about handwriting, for example. The student in question may just be being careless or they may have diagnosed dyspraxia.

Nothing annoys parents and students more than a school apparently ignoring a student's stated special needs. Your TA could and should be the conveyor of this information, and could use a meeting as an opportunity to tell you some of the things that cannot be written down.

A recent example of this was a girl student who became very distressed whilst watching the Gary Sinese's *Of Mice and Men* film at the point when Lennie accidentally kills Curly's wife. It transpired that she had been sexually assaulted by her father. Adequate liaison might have prevented her anguish. The TA might have passed on relevant information about the student. The teacher's outline of the story could then have given warning of any controversial issues.

Part of the TA's brief should be to remind you of such issues while preparing a topic. It is worth remembering that English, together with PHSE and possibly history, are perhaps most prone to dealing with issues which are potentially painful to vulnerable students.

## Roles and responsibilities for TAs

You may or may not have a group of TAs able and willing to discharge the duties outlined above. If not, then the general guidelines in Table 6.1 might help you get off to a good start with your TA. You would obviously adapt them to suit your own circumstances.

**GENERAL GUIDELINES FOR SUPPORT**

| *Avoid* | *Instead* |
|---|---|
| – making decisions for the pupil | – make the choices clear and help pupil to make own decision |
| – sticking relentlessly beside one or two students even if they have a high level of need | – move around the classroom – obviously keeping your main concerns firmly in mind – but be seen to help others |
| – being late! The beginnings of lessons are crucial to the student's understanding and we need you there | – be on time so that you can pick up any misunderstandings or any confusion we might have inadvertently introduced |
| – leaving early! The endings are almost as important | – be there to check misunderstandings about the lesson and any homework |
| – standing there mute! | – don't be afraid to chip in with comments that you think might make the subject clearer. Use our agreed hand signal |
| – letting any students needle you | – make it clear what the consequences are of unacceptable behaviour and inform us |
| – telling the students what to write or say | – use the how, what, where, when and, most crucially, why questions to draw out longer responses |
| – spelling the letters of a word by saying them one by one | – write them down for the student or direct them to use the spell-checker. Get them to record the word in the appropriate place<br>– encourage the student to 'have-a-go' by himself first |
| – acting like a full-time secretary for some of our dyslexic students | – together we need to find a way of making them more independent |
| – telling directly what is wrong with a sentence they have written | – ask them to read the sentence out so they stand more chance of picking it out for themselves |

**Table 6.1** *General Guidelines for Support*

## How to support TAs in developing subject knowledge

Show them the descriptors for the NC levels for En 1, En 2 and En 3. In addition:

- Point out that students are operating at different levels e.g. 2, 3 and 4. Show them the students' work which matches these levels. (This could be an INSET session.)

- Allow them time in the lesson to observe a speaking exchange at various different levels.

- Let them visit other English lessons where higher levels might be on display! See if the department would pay for a TA to attend a coursework moderation meeting. Then you would have a TA that could support a number of different colleagues with the express purpose of supporting coursework.

- Give them time to explore exam board websites to further familiarise themselves with exam criteria.

- If studying AQA English, Oxford University Press market some excellent textbooks such as *Revising AQA English* by Peter Buckroyd, and the *Support Teacher's Book* by Julia Waines. This has been written to directly accompany the AQA English /English Literature Support Book by Joanna Crewe. These books are written in plain language and would be accessible to TAs.

- Allow them to attend moderation/training meetings for Entry Level Certificate. The support materials offered by the WJEC are particularly helpful.

- Ensure that they have a chance to pre-read class reading material!

To nurture a 'specialist' TA in this way will obviously enhance a sense of professionalism and ensure that there is always something constructive for them to do.

Remember also that there is a role for TAs to play in *preparing* pupils for a new topic, as well as in providing extra practice/consolidation.

## Teamwork in managing behaviour

What to do about behaviour? When to intervene or not? Most TAs did not come into the job with the issue of disciplining children uppermost in their mind – indeed we should be very wary of those who do. Sometimes TAs feel that the difficulties that their students face may explain (excuse) their rudeness and abuse, and that putting up with this is part of their job.

Few students have literally no control over their behaviour and even those who have significant behaviour issues should be in possession of a plan in which rudeness and impulsiveness is addressed. If this appears not to be the case, take up the issue with your TA who should be able to tell you whether this is a general problem or indeed one confined to a few curriculum areas – perhaps specifically yours!

Students with literacy difficulties may indeed dread English lessons because they naturally associate them with activities they feel less confident about. Working with your TA, you need to be sure that you are enabling access to appropriate support mechanisms (ICT etc). Students need to know that you are operating as a team and that what is unacceptable to you is by definition also unacceptable to the TA.

Some students will test the role/position of the TA by muttering expletives about you or the TA under their breath. The TA needs to be able to make judgements about whether or not they were intended to hear. The skill of selective deafness can be a useful one to cultivate, but the TA should report the expletive if he or she is in any doubt. It can only reinforce the perception of the class that you are acting as a team. If your TA agonises over the fairness of this, refer them to the analogy of the football referee. They are not always right, but it is vital that they are able to make snap judgements in matters of transgression.

Remind them that it is a useful strategy to offer the students choices when they have hit an impasse – and also to give the student 'take-up' time. This latter strategy is particularly important if the TA has responsibility for just two or three students in the classroom, and should be implemented whenever the TA gives an instruction or a piece of guidance, whether it is mundane – such as 'Jimmy, I would like you to take off your hat, please' – or a written request:

- 'Move away.'

- 'Return shortly to see if the instruction has been carried out.'

- 'Forty-five seconds to a minute at the outside is what is required.'

You may find this proforma useful in formulating your agreement with your assigned Teaching Assistant. We are actually avoiding using the term 'contract' as it seems to be unnecessarily formal.

# Subject Teacher – Support Assistant Agreement

*Guiding principles:*

1. Good teamwork between support staff and class teacher.

2. Joint planning to allow students with SEN to work on the same curriculum area as the rest of the class but at an appropriate level.

3. The support teacher or TA to be supplied with information about work to be attempted.

General aim: To ensure that pupils of all abilities are adequately challenged to solve problems, reflect, formulate strategies and act as independently as possible.

**Subject teacher** . . . . . . . . . . . . . . . . . . **Teaching assistant** . . . . . . . . . . . . . . . . . . .

Teaching group . . . . . . . . . . . . . Subject . . . . . . . . . . . . . . . Room(s) . . . . . . . . . . . . . . . .

Students that are a main focus of support. Indicate level (e.g. SA, SA+, STA) and type of need (e.g. SpLD, EBD, GLD):

Type(s) of support to be offered (please refer to LSS sheet):

Day/time for liaison . . . . . . . . . . . . . . . . Date/time for review . . . . . . . . . . . . . . . . .

**Figure 6.1** *Example of subject teacher/TA agreement*

# Appendices

Appendix 1.1      SEN and Disability Act (SENDA)

Appendix 1.2      Activity 2: What do we really think?

Appendix 2.1      OHT slides for departmental training

Appendix 2.2      Keeping strategies in mind

Appendix 2.3      Draft spelling policy

Appendix 3      Case studies

Appendix 4.1      Turn taking

Appendix 4.2      Talking frames

Appendix 4.3      The Furbles of Tarp (by Charles Cripps)

Appendix 4.4      Lesson plan: using inferential skills and developing predictive skills

Appendix 4.5      Examples from *Macbeth Teaching Pack*

Appendix 4.6      Key word books and spelling policy

Appendix 4.7      Who wants to be a millionaire? Spelling and vocabulary practice

Appendix 4.8      Simplified instructions for starting *Wordbar*

Appendix 4.9      Vocabulary building game

Appendix 4.10      Original writing: *The Assassin* plot, character and setting

Appendix 4.11      Written response to *Macbeth* by William Shakespeare

Appendix 4.12      How to paint a bathroom wall

Appendix 4.13      Lesson plan: fact and opinion

Appendix 4.14      Writing frame for a critical evaluation of a poem

Appendix 4.15      *Jabberwocky* writing frame

Appendix 4.16      Homework ideas

Appendix 5.1      Pupil self-evaluation sheet

Appendix 5.2      Individual education plans

Appendix 6.1      Learning support systems – a description

## SEN and Disability Act 2001 (SENDA)

1   The SEN and Disability Act 2001 amends the Disability Discrimination Act 1995 to include schools' and LEAs' responsibility to provide for pupils and students with disabilities.

2   The definition of a disability in this Act is:
    'someone who has a physical or mental impairment that has an effect on his or her ability to carry out normal day to day activities. The effect must be:
    ● substantial (that is more than minor or trivial); and
    ● long term (that is, has lasted or is likely to last for at least a year or for the rest of the life of the person affected); and
    ● adverse.'

*Activity: List any pupils that you come across that would fall into this category.*

3   The Act states that the responsible body for a school must take such steps as it is reasonable to take to ensure that disabled pupils and disabled prospective pupils are not placed at substantial disadvantage in comparison with those who are not disabled.

*Activity: Give an example of something which might be considered 'a substantial disadvantage'.*

4   The duty on the school to make reasonable adjustments is anticipatory. This means that a school should not wait until a disabled pupil seeks admission to consider what adjustments it might make generally to meet the needs of disabled pupils.

*Activity: Think of two reasonable adjustments that could be made in your school/department.*

5   The school has a duty to plan strategically for increasing access to the school education. This includes provision of information for pupils and parents (e.g. Braille or taped versions of brochures), improving the physical environment for disabled students and increasing access to the curriculum by further differentiation.

*Activity: Consider ways of increasing access to the school for a pupil requesting admission who has Down's Syndrome with low levels of literacy and a heart condition that affects strenuous physical activity.*

6   Schools need to be proactive in seeking out information about a pupil's disability (by establishing good relationships with parents and carers, asking about disabilities during admission interviews, etc.) and ensuring that all staff who might come across the pupil are aware of the pupil's disability.

*Activity: List the opportunities that occur in your school for staff to gain information about disabled students. How can these be improved on?*

## Activity 2: What do we really think?

*Each member of the department should choose two of these statements and pin them on to the noticeboard for an overview of staff opinion. The person leading the session (Head of Department, SENCO, senior manager) should be ready to address any negative feedback and take forward the department with a positive approach.*

If my own child had special needs, I would want her/him to be in a mainstream school mixing with all sorts of kids.

I want to be able to cater for pupils with SEN but feel that I don't have the expertise required.

Special needs kids in mainstream schools are all right up to a point, but I didn't sign up for dealing with the more severe problems – they should be in special schools.

It is the SENCO's responsibility to look out for these pupils with SEN – with help from support teachers.

Pupils with special needs should be catered for the same as any others. Teachers can't pick and choose the pupils they want to teach.

I need much more time to plan if pupils with SEN are going to be coming to my lessons.

Big schools are just not the right places for blind or deaf kids, or those in wheelchairs.

I would welcome more training on how to provide for pupils with SEN in English.

I have enough to do without worrying about kids who can't read or write.

If their behaviour distracts other pupils in any way, youngsters with SEN should be withdrawn from the class.

## OHT slides for departmental training

From *First Steps in Inclusion* (David Fulton Publishers). In the inclusive school:

- classroom climate is considered alongside the curriculum;
- the environment is warm, positive and accepting;
- all students are valued as individuals;
- students learn respect and tolerance for one another;
- students learn ways of working together so everyone can participate.

We should also:

- review the use of peer support and the ways in which students can be involved in developing their own learning programmes;
- consider alternative forms of accreditation at Key Stage 4;
- look at the use of homework across the school.

To work towards becoming more inclusive we must find time:

- to plan together to meet the needs of all students;
- to consider the social effects of pupil groupings;
- to look at the way support is used throughout the school;
- to consider the place of disability awareness in the curriculum.

Definition of an inclusive school (Zemelman 1998):

- more co-operative, collaborative activity
- more in-class support and less withdrawal
- more experimental, hands-on learning
- more responsibility transferred to students for their work
- more mixed ability, less setting and streaming
- more active learning with students doing, talking and collaborating
- more emphasis on learning the key concepts and principles of a subject
- more attention to the emotional needs and varying learning styles of students
- more reliance on teacher's descriptions of progress, less on standardised tests.

## Keeping strategies in mind

| Special Educational Need | Characteristics | Strategies |
|---|---|---|
| Attention Deficit Disorder – with or without hyperactivity | • has difficulty following instructions and completing tasks<br>• easily distracted by noise, movement of others, objects attracting attention<br>• can't stop talking, interrupts others, calls out<br>• acts impulsively without thinking about the consequences | • keep instructions simple – the one sentence rule<br>• make eye contact and use the pupil's name when speaking to him<br>• sit the pupil away from obvious distractions<br>• provide clear routines and rules, rehearse them regularly |
| Autistic Spectrum Disorder | • may experience high levels of stress and anxiety when routines are changed<br>• may have a literal understanding of language<br>• more often interested in objects, rather than people<br>• may be sensitive to light, sound, touch or smell | • give a timetable for each day<br>• warn the pupil about changes to usual routine<br>• avoid using too much eye contact as it can cause distress<br>• use simple, clear language, avoid using metaphor, sarcasm |
| Down's Syndrome | • takes longer to learn and consolidate new skills<br>• limited concentration<br>• has difficulties with thinking, reasoning, sequencing<br>• has better social than academic skills<br>• may have some sight, hearing, respiratory and heart problems | • use simple, familiar language<br>• give time for information to be processed<br>• break lesson up into a series of shorter, varied tasks<br>• accept a variety of ways of recording work, drawings, diagrams, photos, video |
| Hearing Impairment | • may be mild, moderate or severe<br>• may be monoaural, conductive, sensory or mixed loss | • check on the best seating position<br>• check that the pupil can see your face for expressions and lip reading<br>• indicate where a pupil is speaking from during class discussion, only allow one speaker at a time |

| Special Educational Need | Characteristics | Strategies |
|---|---|---|
| Dyscalculia | • has a discrepancy between development level and general ability in maths<br>• has difficulty counting by rote<br>• misses out or reverses numbers<br>• has difficulty with directions, left and right<br>• losing track of turns in games, dance | • provide visual aids, number lines, lists of rules, formulae, words<br>• encourage working out on paper<br>• provide practical objects to aid learning |

## Instructions for activity

This activity should only take about ten minutes but can be used for additional discussion on strategies, concentrating on the easy ones to implement, or the ones already being used.

1. Photocopy onto paper or card.
2. Cut the first column off the sheet.
3. Cut out the remaining boxes.
4. Either keep the two sets of boxes separate, first matching the characteristics then the strategies, or use all together.

Alternative activity: make the boxes bigger with room for additional strategies or remove a couple of the strategies so staff can add any they have used or can identify.

## Draft spelling policy

### Proposed spelling policy

- Use pencil, blue or black ink for correction.

- Underline or highlight the part of the word the student has got wrong.

- Write the word correctly on the same line, underlining or highlighting the bit you have corrected. Instruct the child to write the word correctly at the end of the piece – underlining the letter(s) where the error occurred.

- Focus on subject-specific vocabulary.

- Transfer word to personal dictionary(?)

- No more than five words to be corrected(?)

- Subject-specific vocabulary targeted, especially new words.

- Considerable scope for the basis of homework.

## Case studies

Kuli (male) Y8          Hearing impairment
Harry Y7               Dyslexia
Megan Y10             Wheelchair user
Steven Y8             Emotional, behavioural and social difficulties
Matthew Y9           Cognitive and learning difficulties
Bhavini (female)Y9    Visual impairment
Susan Y10             Complex difficulties, Autistic Spectrum Disorder
Jenny Y7             Down's Syndrome

## Kuli

Kuli has significant hearing loss. He has some hearing in his right ear but is heavily reliant on his hearing aid and visual cues ranging from lip reading to studying body language and facial expression to get the gist and tone of what people are saying. He often misses crucial details. Reading is a useful alternative input and his mechanical reading skills are good but he does not always get the full message because of language delay. He has problems with new vocabulary and with asking and responding to questions.

Now in Year 8, Kuli follows the same timetable as the rest of his class for most of the week but has some individual tutorial sessions with a teacher of the deaf to help with his understanding of the curriculum and to focus on his speech and language development. This is essential but it does mean that he misses some classes, so he is not always up to speed with a subject.

He has a good sense of humour but appreciates visual jokes more than ones which are language based. He is very literal and is puzzled by all sorts of idioms. He was shocked when he heard that someone had been 'painting the town red' as he thought this was an act of vandalism. Even when he knows what he wants to say he does not always have the words or structures to communicate accurately what he knows.

Everyone is very pleasant and quite friendly to him but he is not really part of any group and quite often misunderstands what other pupils are saying. He has a Learning Assistant which again marks him out as different. He gets quite frustrated because he always has ideas that are too complex for his expressive ability. He can be very sulky and has temper tantrums.

### Strategies

- Kuli needs to know what is coming up in the next few lessons so he can prepare the vocabulary, and get some sense of the main concepts so he can follow what is being said. The TA tries to get a list of vital terms from the teacher two days ahead of the lesson.

- The TA to find ways of displaying information visually, using drawings, pictures, signs, symbols, sign language, mime, animations on the computer, etc. Cutting Edge's picture card versions of set texts are always useful.

- Teachers to ensure that they do not stand with their back to the window. (Bright sunlight can dazzle and thus obscure the face and mouth which Kuli relies on for cues.)

- Teachers and students should not shout or exaggerate their 'mouth movements' when communicating with Kuli. This will not help his lip reading.

- The TA to watch out for idiomatic language from the teacher and anticipate possible confusion. This of course may also benefit other classmates.

- The teacher or TA to prepare a *Wordbar* of phrases and vocabulary Kuli might need to prevent him getting frustrated. Pictures from Clip Art files could accompany this grid to help with interpretation. It is possible that the primary version of *Wordbar Clicker 4* might be easier for him to use.

# Kuli's IEP

| Targets | Strategies | Provision | Success Criteria | Achieved |
|---|---|---|---|---|
| 1. To produce pieces of independent writing using Microsoft Word | • Use Word in conjunction with *Wordbar* to provide support with vocabulary. Use grids which provide thesaurus function. | • Use laptop computer in classroom for independent writing.<br>• Use computer at home for homework. | • Three pieces of writing produced independently. | |
| 2. To become more familiar with the use of idiomatic language | • Try EAL material which deals with idiomatic language. | • TA to work with Kuli for 15-minute sessions a week at lunch or registration time.<br>• Try multi-choice format and True/False format. | • Kuli tells English teacher what three idiomatic phrases mean at the end of last English lesson of the week.<br>• Kuli uses some idiomatic phrasing in his writing (four examples in a month). | |
| 3. To increase reading and comprehension skills by six months | • Paired reading with parents.<br>• Use of Successmaker. | • To use Successmaker Reader's Workshop for one or two 12-minute sessions a week in English lessons during period 4 on Fridays with the option to do extra sessions after school. | • Reading and comprehension levels verified by testing. NFER group reading test. | |

| Parent/Carer Involvement: | Pupil's View: | Additional Information: |
|---|---|---|
| Parents wish to buy *Wordbar* licence to support writing.<br>They will hear Kuli read four times a week for 10 minutes. | | |

## Harry

Harry is a very anxious child and although he has now started at secondary school, he still seems to be a 'little boy'. His parents have been very concerned about his slow progress in reading and writing and arranged for a dyslexia assessment when he was eight years old. They also employ a private tutor who comes to the house for two hours per week, and they spend time each evening and at weekends hearing him read and working on phonics with him.

Harry expresses himself well orally, using words which are very sophisticated and adult. His reading is improving (RA 8.4) but his handwriting and spelling are so poor that it is sometimes difficult to work out what he has written. He doesn't just confuse *b* and *d* but also *h* and *y*, *p* and *b*. Increasingly, he uses a small bank of words that he knows he can spell.

His parents want him to be withdrawn from French on the grounds that he should spend extra time on English. The French teacher reports that Harry is doing well with his comprehension and spoken French and is one of the more able children in the class.

Some staff get exasperated with Harry as he is quite clumsy, seems to be in a dream half the time and cannot remember a simple sequence of instructions. He has difficulty telling left from right and so is often talking about the wrong photo or diagram in a book. 'He's just not trying,' said one teacher while others think he needs 'to grow up a bit.'

He is popular with the girls in his class and recently has made friends with some of the boys in the choir.

## Strategies

- Staff to talk to the parents about Harry's lack of confidence. School and parents to seek to identify what Harry does well and to seek ways to acknowledge it and to place his literacy difficulties into the context of just one thing that he is not good at. (Think of all the other things he can do well which other people cannot do as well.) Reward with merit stickers, trips out, etc.

- Try to convince parents that fostering confidence will be likely to create a sea-change in Harry's attitude, and that too much emphasis on what he knows he does badly cannot help matters. Therefore continuing with French for the time being can only be of benefit. He may have a good aural memory.

- Parents to confine nightly reading to Harry's interest areas rather than fiction. Restrict reading time to 10–15 minutes each night at time to be mutually agreed, i.e. not to clash with favourite television programme. English teacher to engage with Harry in discussion about what he has read on a regular basis, and recommend 'good' books. Feedback to school for additional praise on a job well done.

- Provide Harry with strategies for distinguishing left from right. Encourage him to think of the reading direction (left to right) and that L comes before R in the alphabet. The word 'LetteR' has Left and Right in the right positions. Pictorial representation might work for Harry for his problem letters. Get him to curl the index finger of each hand to meet with his thumb and ask him to straighten the rest. He then has a 'b' and a 'd' in the right alphabet order. (This will help him with left and right as well.)

- Pictographic ways of showing 'h', 'y' and 'p' can follow later. (He may be familiar with the pictogram methods of Lyn Wendon's Letterland system from earlier school days. Discreet reminders of these ideas might be beneficial.)

- Find out how he has learnt things and see if similar strategies would work in the classroom. *Timely Reminders* computer program from Jane Mitchell (Communication and Learning Skills Centre – CALSC) might help here.

- If he has a computer, suggest he makes use of the strategies for dealing with spelling outlined in Chapter 4, 'The Inclusive Classroom'. Investigate the possibility of using a computer with spellchecker at home and school to cope with orthographic and spelling difficulties. He should particularly use the autocorrect facility and the thesaurus.

- Use of a Dictaphone to take notes. Cheap ones taking standard cassettes can be bought from organisations such as ianSYST. Avoid masses of note taking or copying from the board (good practice anyway!).

- Suggest airline pilot style checklist for books and equipment to be done the night before school.

- Concentrate on the introduced vocabulary in a particular lesson for marking purposes.

- Use of *Wordbar*, predictive word processors, voice activated speech.

## Harry's IEP

| Targets | Strategies | Provision | Success Criteria | Achieved |
|---|---|---|---|---|
| **1.** Provide Harry with strategies for distinguishing left from right | • Think of the reading direction (left to right) and that L comes before R. The word 'LetteR' has Left and Right in the right positions. | • Use index finger of each hand to create 'b' and a 'd' in the right alphabet order. | • Harry gets his 'b' and 'd' correct most of the time by the end of term (90% correct). | |
| **2.** To be able to spell a further 10 NLS words both in isolation and context | • To learn three–five new words each week.<br>• To revise Look Cover Write check system.<br>• To look for short words in longer words to help him spell. | • Construct a personal word bank to accompany his writing.<br>• Colour code the difficult bits. | • Harry gets all of his NLS words correct by testing at the end of each week.<br>• Shows confidence in using his word bank in English lessons. | |
| **3.** To produce more readable handwriting | • Use of peer support to identify neat letter formation.<br>• Unjoining 'tailed' letters.<br>• Peer to provide running reminders in lesson time. | • Experimentation to find most suitable pen.<br>• TA to check that all basic equipment is present (ruler, pencil, etc.) | • Handwriting/presentation skills improve by Easter.<br>• Peer and TA both agree with Harry's judgement! | |

**Parent/Carer Involvement:**
To support Harry's drive to improve his presentation skills and to monitor his use of the computer at home. They will keep an eye out for his 'b' and 'd'.
They will check his spelling on his personal word bank.

**Pupil's View:**

**Additional Information:**

## Megan

Everyone knows when Megan is around! She is very outgoing, loud and tough. No one feels sorry for her – they wouldn't dare! Megan has spina bifida and needs a wheelchair and personal care as well as educational support. She has upset a number of the less experienced Classroom Assistants who find her a 'real pain'. Some of the teachers like her because she is very sparky. If she likes a subject, she works hard – or at least she did until this year.

Megan has to be up very early for her parents to help get her ready for school before the bus comes at 7.50 a.m. She lives out of town and is one of the first to be picked up and one of the last to be dropped off, so she has a longer school day than many of her classmates. Tiredness can be a problem as everything takes her so long to do and involves so much effort.

Now she is fifteen, she has started working towards her GCSEs and has the potential to get several A to Cs particularly in maths and sciences. She is intelligent but is in danger of becoming disaffected because everything is so much harder for her than for other children. Recently she has lost her temper with a teacher, made cruel remarks to a very sensitive child, and turned her wheelchair round so she sat with her back to a supply teacher. She has done no homework for the last few weeks saying that she doesn't see the point as 'no one takes a crip seriously'.

## Strategies

- Challenge her view about nobody taking a 'crip' seriously. Look at role models from the disabled world.

- Ask for her help in hearing younger children read or resolving learning difficulties for them. This might help her become a little less introspective.

- Urgent support is needed to minimise the physical effort involved in writing and recording. She needs as much independence as possible – so she needs access to predictive word-processors or, better still, voice-activated word-processors such as Dragon Dictate or IBM's Via Voice. This should be available on a laptop for her personal use.

- When she wants to word-process, the use of the sticky key feature might help her. This will hold down certain keys such as Caps Lock and Control so she only has to use one hand when she is feeling tired.

- She needs to be at the centre of the decision-making process about arrangements that affect her. She needs to have the sense that people are doing things *with* her and not *to* her.

- Establish ground rules about behaviour. She needs to understand that while the school is sympathetic to her, rudeness is not acceptable whatever the circumstances.

- A behaviour contract drawn up with her full co-operation and agreement might be appropriate. A 'traffic light' routine might help her – where she 'stops' before she says or does something, then 'thinks' about the consequences, and then 'does'.

- Have higher expectations of her. Remind her of what she can do and how well she has responded to the challenge of her circumstances so far. Remind her that she has no real option but to continue to fight.

- Introduce her to relevant literature such as Christy Moore's *My Left Foot* and more recently *The Curious Incident of the Dog in the Night Time* about the imagined experiences of a boy with Asperger's Syndrome.

- Suggest that she joins a poetry writing group either within or outside of school. To avoid fatigue suggest that she concentrates on short forms such as haiku and cinquains. Praise her efforts and display her work.

## Megan's IEP

| Targets | Strategies | Provision | Success Criteria | Achieved |
|---|---|---|---|---|
| 1. To produce pieces of independent writing using Word | • Use Microsoft Word in conjunction with *Wordbar* to provide support with spelling and structuring writing. | • Use computer as base for independent writing – all subjects.<br>• Use computer at home for homework.<br>• Support from TA when free. | • Three pieces of writing produced independently. | |
| 2. To produce pieces of independent writing using voice-activated word processor | • Use Word in conjunction with head microphone voice-activated word processor. Provide support with spelling and structuring writing. | • Loan use of laptop with headphones in English classroom. | • Megan manages the computer and headset effectively. | |
| 3. To consider the consequences of what she says and how she says it. | • A 'traffic light' routine to try: she 'stops' before she says or does something (red), then 'thinks' about the consequences (amber), and then 'does' (green). | • Possible picture of traffic lights to remind her. | • Review at end of week to consider successful implementation of scheme. Recount situations in which strategy has worked. | |

**Parent/Carer Involvement:**
Provision of *Wordbar* licence for use at home. Possible provision of voice-activated word processor to use at home. Oversight of its use.

**Pupil's View:**

**Additional Information:**
Remember to address the 'adult' in Megan when talking to her.

# Steven

'Stevie' is a real charmer – sometimes! He is totally inconsistent: one day he is full of enthusiasm; the next day he is very tricky and he needs to be kept on target. He thrives on attention. In primary school, he spent a lot of time sitting by the teacher's desk and seemed to enjoy feeling special. If he sat there he would get on with his work, but then as soon as he moved to sit with his friends he wanted to make sure he was the centre of attention.

Now in Year 8, Steven sometimes seems lazy – looking for the easy way out – but at other times he is quite dynamic and has lots of bright ideas. He can't work independently and has a very short attention span. No one has very high expectations of him and he is not about to prove them wrong.

Some of the children don't like him because he can be a bully but really he is not nasty. He is a permanent lieutenant for some of the tougher boys and does things to win their approval.

He is a thief but mostly he takes silly things, designed to annoy rather than for any monetary value. He was found with someone's library ticket and stole one shoe from the changing rooms during PE.

Since his mother began a relationship with a new partner, there has been a deterioration in behaviour and Steven has also been cautioned by police after stealing from a local DIY store. He has just been suspended for throwing a chair at a teacher, but staff suspect this was because he was on a dare. He certainly knows how to get attention.

## Strategies

- Structured programme with lots of rewards – certificates, merits, etc. Weekly targets to be closely tied to tangible rewards granted by mother – phone credit, Macdonald's visits, favourite chocolate bar, etc.

- Weekly feedback to mother giving a résumé of the week by the same person. Steven will know that this is part of the deal.

- At the beginning of the week Steven to consider the previous week on a scale of one to ten. Whatever the figure, even if it is low (say 2/10), Steven to consider what had gone right to merit that figure. Then to set a numerical target for the coming week and then consider what he has to do to meet the figure. This process can obviously be done by the English department alone and it might be particularly relevant if English is a particular battleground.

- Sit Steven where the teacher can easily ascertain that he is attending. This may be at the front of the class but should be away from doors, windows, heaters, etc. which might prove a distraction. Focus on success to build confidence.

- Information and tasks to be delivered in short chunks or 'one at a time' to avoid overload – but make it clear to Steven how many chunks there are at the outset so he cannot get the impression that there can be no end in sight.

- Sanction the use of something that he can officially 'fiddle with' while waiting for or listening to instructions, e.g. a 'stress buster'. The 'thing' is mutually agreed between the teacher and Steven. Steven to choose and teacher to approve. This may ultimately help his concentration.

- Keep the classroom routine consistent as far as possible, or if a major departure is anticipated (such as re-arranging furniture to hold a class debate), Steven will be told about this in good time so that he may anticipate the new activity.

- Make sure there are lots of changes of activity.

- Give him some responsibility, such as handing out papers or putting books away, which will increase self-esteem and also help to reduce the amount of time that Steven must sit in one spot. The physical movement will help to focus his attention.

- Teaching staff to attempt to engage him in conversation about his interests as he enters the classroom to establish positive atmosphere.

- If Steven manages to put his hand up appropriately, the teacher will attempt to answer him as quickly as possible as he will not have the patience to wait.

- Steven and his teacher to decide on a signal which will signify that his attention is required, such as a hand signal – or a long stare!

- Steven will try and employ the 'Stop-Think-Go' traffic light principle to help him think of the consequences of his actions before he is tempted to do something he will later regret. He will carry a laminated picture of a traffic light post labelled 'Stop-Think-Go' which he will put out on his desk before the lesson starts.

# Steven's IEP

| Targets | Strategies | Provision | Success Criteria | Achieved |
|---------|-----------|-----------|------------------|----------|
| 1. To consider the consequences of what he says and how he says it | • A 'traffic light' routine to try: he 'stops' before he says or does something (red), then 'thinks' about the consequences (amber), and then 'does' (green). | • Picture of traffic lights to place on desk to remind him.<br>• Meeting with TA to set up for week – identify potential troublespots/lessons in week. | • Review at end of week to consider successful implementation of scheme. Recount situations in which strategy has worked. | |
| 2. To maintain a positive outlook on achievements | • Rate week in terms of a score out of 10.<br>• Analyse what went right to account for the score. | • TA and tutor to praise and note. Keep a track of cumulative scores.<br>• English teacher to note periods of time he is on task – reward/feedback to tutor increased periods of concentration.<br>• Tutor to feed back success stories to Mum at end of each week. | • Steven to recognise achievements.<br>• To decide for himself what he has to do/what he has to change to improve on his score for the following week.<br>• Steven meets targets he has set for himself. | |
| 3. To produce pieces of independent writing using Word | • Use Microsoft Word in conjunction with *Wordbar* to provide support with spelling and structuring writing.<br>• Steven delivered tasks one at a time – knowing in advance how many components there are. | • Use computer as base for independent writing – all subjects.<br>• Use computer at home for homework.<br>• Support from TA when free. | • Three pieces of writing produced independently with maximum of one reminder to stay on task. | |

| Parent/Carer Involvement: | Pupil's View: |
|---------------------------|---------------|
| To reward Stevie with phone credits if he meets his targets for the week.<br><br>To arrange to take phone messages from tutor. | |

**Additional Information:**

Steven allowed to 'fiddle' with small squidgy rubber ball while listening.

# Matthew

Matt is a very passive boy. He has no curiosity, no strong likes or dislikes. One teacher said, 'He's the sort of boy who says yes to everything to avoid further discussion, but I sometimes wonder if he understands anything.'

Now in Year 9, he is quite a loner. He knows all the children and does not feel uncomfortable with them but is always on the margins. Often in class he sits and does nothing, just stares into space. He is no trouble and indeed if there is any kind of conflict, he absents himself or ignores it. No one knows very much about him as he never volunteers any information. He once said that he had a dog and one teacher has seen him on the local common with a terrier but no one is sure if it is his.

He does every piece of work as quickly as possible to get it over with. His work is messy and there is no substance to anything he does which makes it hard for teachers to suggest a way forward, or indeed to find anything to praise. Matthew often looks a bit grubby and is usually untidy. He can be quite clumsy and loses things regularly but does not bother to look for them. He does less than the acceptable minimum.

## Strategies

- Get parents/carers in to find out if he has any enthusiasms at home. Investigate possible interest in dogs. If he has, refer and respond to these as he enters the classroom to demonstrate interest in him. If he has not, establish what Matthew's routine is at home and how much time parents are able to spend with him.

- Encourage parents to find time to take him out to stimulating places, preferably with at least one friend.

- Involve him in pair work with a carefully chosen livelier pupil (a girl), who will periodically remind him to stay on task.

- Set up situations in small groups where he can make a contribution. TA and/or peer tutor to encourage Matthew to explain, discuss, and apply information he has just read.

- Ask Matthew to 'teach' facts or ideas he has learned from his non-fiction reading to English teacher – especially from an interest area.

- Set up some one-to-one sessions with a TA where Matthew is pushed to respond.

- Get him using technology to improve the appearance of his work, perhaps in a homework club after school. Encourage use of PowerPoint and Publisher programs.

- Try Matthew with digital photography which might stimulate a new interest and encourage more pride in his work as he learns to integrate this with his written work.

- Try playing some word games with a small group. Try crossword puzzles, word bingo, Scrabble®, or Boggle®. These will build vocabulary and word understanding as well as providing a context for social integration.

- Get an older student to do some paired reading with Matthew, thus encouraging him to read aloud every day. Matthew should continue this process at home.

- Encourage Matthew to develop 'to do' lists. Help to monitor partner's books and vice versa. Get him to use Outlook program for his lists.

## Matthew's IEP

| Targets | Strategies | Provision | Success Criteria | Achieved |
|---|---|---|---|---|
| 1. To make more oral contributions in English lessons | • Pair with Tracy Scroggins to 'snowball' ideas. Tracy to encourage Matthew to share them with the group. | • Tracy and Matthew to meet with English teacher to agree ground rules regarding the snowball technique and how much Matthew is to contribute. | • Matthew keeps to agreement and volunteers oral contributions. | |
| 2. To produce pieces of independent writing using Microsoft Word, PowerPoint and Publisher | • Use Word in conjunction with *Wordbar* to provide support with spelling and structuring writing.<br>• Use PowerPoint in conjunction with digital pictures to foster pride in his work. | • Training from peer or sixth former in how to use PowerPoint and Publisher.<br>• Be part of a group that learns to use a digital camera.<br>• Use computer at home for homework. | • Three pieces of writing produced independently that make sense all the way through.<br>• Confident and independent use of the technology. | |
| 3. To become better organised | • Develop 'to do' lists.<br>• Use 'pilot style' checklists to accompany each day of the week. | • Use sixth form mentor as support to guide Matthew in use of organisational techniques.<br>• Investigate use of Outlook 'To Do' lists on computer. | • Matthew begins to take initiative for organising his equipment.<br>• All agree by Easter that matters have improved. | |

| Parent/Carer Involvement:<br>To support Matthew's organisational efforts at home.<br>To encourage him to pursue his possible interest in dogs (attend shows, training classes etc). | Pupil's View: |
|---|---|

**Additional Information:**
Keep a discreet eye on Matthew – praise and reward any efforts to participate. He needs lots of encouragement.

# Bhavini

Bhavini has very little useful sight. She uses a stick to get around school and some of the other children make cruel comments about this which she finds very hurtful. She also wears glasses with thick lenses which she hates. On more than one occasion, she has been knocked over in the corridor, but she insists that these incidents were accidents and that she is not being bullied. However, her sight is so poor she may not recognise pupils who pick on her.

She has a certain amount of specialist equipment such as talking scales in food technology and a CCTV for text books, but now in Year 9, she is always conscious of being different. Her classmates accept her but she is very cut off as she does not make eye contact or see well enough to find people she knows to sit with at break. She spends a lot of time hanging around the support area. Her form tutor has tried to get other children to take her under their wing or to escort her to Humanities, which is in another building, but this has bred resentment. She has friends outside school at the local Phab club (Physically handicapped/able bodied) and has taken part in regional VI athletics tournaments, although she opts out of sport at school if she can. Some of the teachers are concerned about health and safety issues and there has been talk about her being disapplied from science.

She has a reading age approximately three years behind her chronological age and spells phonetically. Many of the teaching strategies used to make learning more interesting tend to disadvantage her. The lively layout of her French book with cartoons and speech bubbles is a nightmare. Even if she has a page on her CCTV or has a photocopy of the text enlarged she cannot track which bit goes where. At the end of one term she turned up at the support base asking for some work to do because 'they're all watching videos'.

## Strategies

- Her isolation is the key factor and needs addressing most urgently. Recruit an older student/sixth former to act as a mentor and a mediator between Bhavini and her peers.

- Students can experience the degree of poor vision Bhavini has by wearing specially adapted glasses and then trying to negotiate the school classroom. The group then articulates what they feel are the practical difficulties Bhavini faces and endeavours to offer some solutions. This could be an oral exercise in the context of English, i.e. a practical consideration of the language demands required to guide someone around the classroom by voice commands alone. Bhavini to advise on good and not so good performances.

- Students to understand that Bhavini may be unable to detect mood from facial expressions and will simply appear to ignore them because she doesn't see them! It will also be difficult for her to detect the appropriate point to make her own oral contribution as we often rely on visual clues to tell us when someone is about to finish speaking.

- Bhavini to examine the way she talks to her peers. Does she seem to treat them like servants? Does she seem off-hand? What is her tone like when she is talking? Does she make an effort to engage in the interests of others? This can be very difficult to do when life is so hard within school – but effort placed in this area might later pay dividends.

- She needs to be put in groups with different pupils who will not overwhelm her. Bhavini will work with her sixth form mentor to establish who might fit the bill in her peer group.

- It is vital to establish effective liaison regarding the practical difficulties Bhavini will face on a week-by-week basis. The school should investigate using the projector for her classes when videos are to be shown.

- The school might like to experiment with brightly coloured tape 'way markers' on the corridor walls to help guide Bhavini to her next class. This might help cut down her dependence on others. This could be a project for ASDAN, GNVQ or BTEC students.

- Build up a core and subject-specific vocabulary word bank. Take key words into the lesson in size 48 point font.

- Investigate the purchase of specialist ICT programs that enlarge the text on the computer screen. These tend to be expensive so it may be worth applying to 'Ability Net' for help with funding.

- In the meantime, Bhavini might like to experiment with the 'magnifier' program supplied with Microsoft Windows 2000 and above. This might have the effect of isolating bits of text which might make it easier for her to deal with. She would additionally be helped by using a larger monitor.

- In conjunction, Bhavini should try different fonts for ease of reading and avoid fixed space fonts that may be more difficult to read. A plain font, with sans serif letters, is often easier to read.

- She should be able to change the shape and size of a mouse pointer and also show 'mouse trails' which make it easier to find the cursor on the screen. She might be able to call upon a range of sounds which can warn a sight-impaired user when they use certain commands.

- Experiment with voice-activated programs such as Dragon Dictate or Via Voice in conjunction with some others.

- Bhavini could usefully develop her keyboard skills. There is a range of software programs available to help learners. (See Becta Educational Software Database: http://besd.becta.org.uk/). The Royal National Institute for the Blind (RNIB) 'Accessing Technology' website provides helpful guide to the development of keyboard skills: http://www.rnib.org.uk/technology/factsheets/keyboard.htm#keyboard

- TA to disentangle lively text faces so that tasks are presented in a logical, bullet-pointed, step by step, 'one after the other' manner. Bhavini to advise on what colour background suits her best.

- Bhavini might like to experiment with an overlay keyboard which could provide her with a combination of sensory stimuli. It is possible to create tactile overlays, which can enhance access when used with speech feedback or visual representation.

- TA or sixth form support can arrange for text to be scanned into a computer. It can then be enlarged on screen and 'read' aloud by a speech synthesiser attached to the computer, such as those supplied with TextHELP's *Read and Write* and Don Johnston's *Co-Writer*.

- The advanced versions of the above programs are able to read Internet websites – so Bhavini can explore the RNIB website and others while looking for independent means of seeking support. She might find the following useful:

## Organisations

British Computer Association of the Blind (BCAB): http://www.bcab.org.uk

National Listening Library: http://www.listening-books.org.uk

Inclusive Technology provides information and pointers to resources on ICT and visual impairment: http://www.inclusive.co.uk/infosite/snhome.shtml

The RNIB produces an annual guide to hardware and software available to support pupils with visual impairment. The latest edition, *Accessing Technology*, concentrates on the application of ICT as well as listing devices and manufacturers: http://www.rnib.org.uk/technology/welcome.htm

## Bhavani's IEP

| Targets | Strategies | Provision | Success Criteria | Achieved |
|---|---|---|---|---|
| 1. To improve keyboard skills | • Four 15-minute sessions a week developing keyboard skills. | • Advice from RNIB and advisory teacher regarding appropriate programs. | • Bhavini feels confident in use of the keyboard and her typing speed has significantly increased. | |
| 2. To build up a core and subject-specific vocabulary word bank | • Select two or three of the spellings that Bhavini needs to use in her writing and needs to learn to spell. | • Spelling print-out specific to each subject.<br>• Mnemonics.<br>• *TextHelp* and *Woodbar* programs.<br>• Use Look/Say/Write/Cover/Check routine. | • Greater confidence at accuracy noted by April. | |
| 3. For Bhavini to feel more confident and included with her peers | • Mentor to spend time with her and to act as mediator with her peers.<br>• Bhavini to think carefully about how she speaks to others. | • Meeting with mentor at the beginning and end of the week.<br>• Session with TA to examine the tone of her speech and meanings others might derive from it. | • Bhavini is seen to be more included in the class dynamics by Easter. | |

| Parent/Carer Involvement:<br>Parents to help support her learning of core vocabulary for four 10-minute sessions a week. | Pupil's View: | Additional Information:<br>Watch carefully for any sign of teasing from her peers. Deal with it discreetly but firmly. |
|---|---|---|

## Susan

Susan is a tall, very attractive girl who has been variously labelled as having Asperger's and 'cocktail party syndrome'. She talks fluently but usually about something totally irrelevant. She is very charming and her language is sometimes quite sophisticated, but her ability to use language for school work in Year 10 operates at a much lower level. Her reading is excellent on some levels but she cannot draw inferences from the printed word. If you ask her questions about what she has read, she looks blank, echoes what you have said, looks puzzled or changes the subject – something she is very good at.

She finds relationships quite difficult. She is very popular, especially with the boys in her class. They think she is a laugh. There have been one or two problems with some of the boys in school. Her habit of standing too close to people and her over-familiarity have led to misunderstandings which have upset her. Her best friend, Laura, is very protective of her and tries to mother her, to the extent of doing some of her work for her so she won't get into trouble.

Her work is limited. In art all her pictures look the same: very small cramped drawings. She does not like to use paint because 'it's messy'. She finds it very hard to relate to the wider world and sees everything in terms of her own experience. The class has been studying *Macbeth* and she has not moved beyond saying, 'I don't believe in witches and ghosts'.

Some teachers think she is being wilfully stupid or not paying attention. She seems to be attention-seeking as she is very poor at turn-taking and shouts out in class if she thinks of something to say or wants to know how to spell a word. When she was younger, she used to retreat under the desk when she was upset and had to be coaxed out. She is still easily offended and cannot bear being teased. She has an answer for everything and while it may not be sensible or reasonable, there is an underlying logic.

## Strategies

- Ascertain how much Susan knows about her condition. Has the term Asperger's Syndrome been explained to her? What are her parents' wishes? It is *vital* to know the status of her knowledge! If she is fully aware of her situation, encourage her to read *The Strange Case of the Dog in the Night Time* to see how much of the boy's situation she recognises in herself.

- Recruit Laura as a peer tutor. Enter a formal agreement whereby both agree that it is no help to Susan in the long term if everything is done for her. Laura to warn her when she is going off task (a picture sign might be appropriate). This could be backed up by a teacher signal. Weekly meetings with the TA and the teacher to chart when and where this is happening. Tangible rewards when Laura reports that Susan stayed on task.

- Laura and Susan to agree not to sit next to each other for some lessons in the week to help Susan develop some independence. To start with *one* lesson in the week. Both girls to be positioned out of each other's sight line.

- Try the Literacy catch-up unit *Reading between the lines* to see if this helps with her very poor inferential skills. (Deliverable by TA as it is very prescriptive.)

- Provide writing frames and model answers she can base her work on – particularly those that require an inferential response. Try a series of prompt questions which might lead her to the appropriate response.

- Discussion of social issues, body language, appropriate behaviour. Susan needs to clearly appreciate what boys will assume given certain cues, e.g. standing very close, touching, etc. She will need to accept this as a fact even though she probably will not understand it. This may need to be written on cue cards to serve as a reminder.

## Susan's IEP

| Targets | Strategies | Provision | Success Criteria | Achieved |
|---|---|---|---|---|
| 1. For Susan to develop more classroom independence | • Use friend Laura as peer tutor – to warn her when she is going off task. | • Agreed sign between the two as warning device.<br>• Laura not to sit next to Susan one English lesson out of three. | • Susan stays on task and takes note of warning.<br>• Susan becomes less dependent on Laura. | |
| 2. For Susan to develop some inferential skills | • Model alternative explanations beyond the straightforward.<br>• Get Susan to copy the procedure. | • DfES literacy catch-up unit *Reading between the lines* delivered by TA for 20 minutes for part of one English lesson a week.<br>• TA to relate procedures to set texts currently being studied.<br>• Use of guidance writing frames. | Susan works her way through five of the lessons and understands them. | |
| 3. For Susan to think about the consequences of her actions. | • To adopt the stop-think-go strategy before she acts.<br>• Training in the inferences others will draw from her oral and body language. | • Pictorial traffic lights to remind her.<br>• Cue cards to remind her of what might happen if she stands too close, touches too freely, etc. | • Much reduced incidents involving boys. | |

**Parent/Carer Involvement:**
Parents to support her inferential skills training. They will help with prompt questions and sentence starters.

**Pupil's View:**

**Additional Information:**
Susan probably has Asperger's Syndrome and has great difficulty understanding things beyond the literal.

Be aware of the potential social difficulties Susan might get herself into. Watch for 'boy trouble'.

## Jenny

Jenny is in Year 7 and has Down's Syndome. She is a very confident child who has been cherished and encouraged by her mother and older brothers and sisters. She is very assertive and is more than capable of dealing with spiteful comments – 'I don't like it when you call me names. You're cruel and I hate you' – but this assertiveness can lead to obstinacy. She is prone to telling teachers that they are wrong!

She has average skills in reading and writing but her work tends to be unimaginative and pedestrian. She enjoys biology but finds the rest of the science curriculum hard going. She has started to put on weight and tries to avoid PE. She has persuaded her mother to provide a note saying that she tires easily but staff know that she is a bundle of energy and is an active member of an amateur theatre group which performs musicals. She has a good singing voice and enjoys dancing.

She went to a local nursery and primary school and fitted in well. She always had some one to sit next to and was invited to all the best birthday parties. Teachers and other parents frequently praised her and she felt special.

Now in secondary school, everything has changed. Some of her friends from primary school have made new friendships and don't want to spend so much time with her. She is very hurt by this and feels excluded. She is also struck by how glamorous some of the older girls look and this has made her more self-conscious.

## Strategies

- English is a relative 'strength' – so give her lots of opportunities to succeed.

- Provide stimulatory experiences prior to any creative work (see Chapter 4).

- Teacher or TA to visit a production of the amateur theatre group of which she is a member – possibly with a peer supporter. Enlist the support of director to encourage her to join equivalent school-based groups.

- Encourage new groupings in class so she gets to meet other children from different feeder schools. She could also be part of an induction team to welcome new students to the school.

- Pair her up with a child who has better imaginative/empathy skills but weaker literacy so they can support each other.

- Encourage Jenny to keep a diary which records her thoughts and feelings. She can then discuss relevant details with an older student or supportive peer who is perhaps keeping his/her own diary.

- If there is a creative writing/poetry group, encourage her to join.

- Staff need to be aware that Jenny is likely to be increasingly left behind by her peers as she goes up through the secondary system, and that differentiation is likely to increasingly be an issue.

- Help her to understand the consequences of what she may say to others. Give her option choices to choose from when faced with a particular situation, e.g. 'If you say you hate Emma, she is likely to: a) be frightened b) be sorry c) tease you more.'

- Show her the difference between assertive, aggressive and passive responses to particular situations. Lucky Duck publications produce useful resources which might help her.

## Jenny's IEP

| Targets | Strategies | Provision | Success Criteria | Achieved |
|---|---|---|---|---|
| 1. Improve Jenny's social integration within the group | • Meet other children from different feeder schools.<br>• Be part of induction team welcoming new students and visitors. | • Encourage new groupings in class.<br>• Social skills training as part of the induction group to deal with visitors. | • Jenny feels that her sense of personal usefulness has grown by Easter. | |
| 2. Improve Jenny's success at working within a pair | • Mutual support. Jenny helps someone with inferior literacy skills. | • Partner helps Jenny with imaginative ideas and can suggest the right things to say in a given situation. | • Jenny and partner demonstrate that they can help each other.<br>• Jenny has tangibly helped peer with decoding reading requirements. | |
| 3. Improve Jenny's reflective and predictive abilities | • Encourage the keeping of a diary and the writing of poetry to a given formula. | • Jenny joins a school-based creative writing group.<br>• Learns about the structure of Haiku and Cinquian poetic forms. | • Jenny enjoys writing and feels that it helps her deal with the tribulations of day-to-day life. | |

**Parent/Carer Involvement:**
Seek help with regard to Susan's eating habits.
Help to guide her in improved dress sense.

**Pupil's View:**

**Additional Information:**
Staff to be aware that the gap between her and her peers is likely to widen with the years. Watch out for teasing and for Jenny's potential retaliation.

## Turn taking

- Listen to the speaker and think about what he is saying.

- Look at the speaker – he may pause and look at you and expect you to speak.

- Wait until the speaker has finished what he is saying before you speak – even if you think you can guess what he is going to say.

- Be fair – everyone should have a chance to speak.

- Keep it short – don't carry on too long – let someone else have a say.

# Talking frames

## Adapted from *Speaking Frames* by Sue Palmer; David Fulton Publishers

Talking frames were originally devised to help children get to grips with written language, though their potential for the development of student's oral language skills is perhaps even more important.

Many students find speaking in front of an audience difficult. Their natural spoken language may be fragmented, incoherent, with limited vocabulary and lacking in organisation. Speaking frames provide support in translating their ideas into coherent sentences, and preparing their presentation gives the time to consider vocabulary, develop explicitness and experiment with more formal connectives than they would usually use. Practice makes perfect, and opportunities to practise presentation skills should also develop children's confidence, social skills and self-esteem.

## How speaking frames work

In pairs, groups or as individuals, pupils work on a specific task and fit their answers into a given frame for oral presentation to the class. The class therefore *listens* to a number of presentations based on the frame:

- first by the teacher, as he or she demonstrates the process

- next by more able pupils, selected by the teacher as likely to provide good and fluent models

- then by their remaining peers

And every student has an opportunity to *imitate* and *innovate* on the same language patterns as they make their own presentation.

Paired work is the easiest type of speaking frame presentation. Students who have previously used a 'talking partners' technique should adjust to using frames quickly; for those who have not used the technique, the frames are an ideal introduction. This approach helps pupils to report on their work in more formal 'literate language' than they would usually use. This gives them the chance to hear this language issuing from their own mouths, prior (it is to be hoped) to using it in written work, and to develop their control of a wider vocabulary.

The frames specifically cover these aspects of literate talk:

- speaking in complete sentences

- varying sentence construction (including a variety of sentence openings – adverbials, subordinate clauses)

- the standard English '. . . and I' (as opposed to 'Me and . . .')

- the language of exemplication (*such as, for instance, for example*)

- 'literate' connectives (*however, also, on the whole*)

They can be used for work with all types of text, with the emphasis adjusted to suit the ability of individual students and the particular aims of the lesson.

## Example 1

Before using this speaking frame, children should know how to approach a piece of research by brainstorming under the headings:

- What do we know?

- What do we need to know?

- How will we find out?

If this has been taught through class lessons, this paired activity is a useful follow-up task.

---

'**Hannah** and I are researching **Anne Frank**.

We already know that **she lived during the Second World War and had to hide from the Nazi soldiers**.

We also know **that she wrote a diary about it**.

However, we think we ought to know more about **how she and her family managed to hide and survive, who helped them and how long they were hidden**.

It might also help to find out **what happened in the end. We think she died but we don't know how or when**.

To find out more about our topic we are going to start by **looking in the school library for books about Anne Frank or the Second World War**.

We could also try **looking up Anne Frank on the internet, and in encyclopaedias**.'

---

Talk about:

- the ways in which the speaking frame avoids repetitive sentence structures (in reporting back something of this kind, most children would begin every sentence in the same way, e.g. *We found some . . ., We scanned . . ., We spotted . . .*)

- useful connectives, e.g. *however* and *also*

## Example 2

Before using this speaking frame, students should know how to appraise the usefulness of a non-fiction book for their research by:

- scanning contents list, headings, captions, etc;

- checking key words in the index;

- checking the age of the book through the copyright date.

If all this has been taught through class lessons, this paired activity provides a useful follow-up task.

---

'**Mahinder** and I are researching **Anne Frank, who was a girl who wrote a diary about hiding from the Nazis in the Second World War.**

We chose this book called **Children in the Second World War.**

It is by **Kenna Bourke** and was published in **2003.**

In the Contents we found out some useful chapter headings such as **Anne Frank** and **Anne Frank's Diary.**

When we scanned through the book we noticed other items that might help. For instance **on page 7 there is a picture of Anne, with a caption that said 'Jews like Anne Frank were forced into hiding'. We kept an eye open for more about Jews and found something about Jewish children on page 33.**

In the index we spotted some key words that might be useful to us, including **Anne Frank, Jews and Nazis. We also found some other places to look in the Bibliography, including Anne's diary and a good website.**'

---

Talk about:

- the 'technical language' associated with books, e.g. *copyright, index, contents, headings, captions*;

- the language used to introduce examples (*such as, for instance, including*);

- the use of the word *items*. This can be a useful substitute for the looser word *things* that children tend to use;

- using the book as a visual aid for the talk and perhaps pointing to relevant pages/features as they refer to them.

## Example 3

Before using this speaking frame, students should know how to analyse the organisation and content of a sequence of paragraphs in a non-fiction book:

- Read the passage through to get an overview.

- Highlight or underline key words in each paragraph.

- Summarise the content of the paragraph in a single sentence.

If these skills have been taught through class lessons, the paired task is an ideal consolidation activity.

---

'**Hannah** and I have been reading this passage about **Anne Frank.** It consists of **three paragraphs and a short picture story.**

The first paragraph is **an introduction about how Hitler treated Jewish people and how some people helped them. Some of the key words are** *Hitler, Jewish people, dangerous, imprisoned, murdered, families, tried to help, punished or killed, a million and a half Jewish children died.*

The next paragraph is about **how some Jewish families hid in Holland and other countries, and how hard their lives were. Key words here include** *constant danger, lived in secret, never went out, relying on other people.*

The third paragraph **summarises what happened to Anne Frank. Some key words are** *famous, Holland, Holocaust, family and four others, two years, rooms above office, Amsterdam.*

The final **part of the passage is a picture story with captions telling about Anne's life. The key words are** *1933 aged 4, Amsterdam; school, new friends; 1940 Hitler invaded Holland; 1942 hiding, rooms above office; 1944 Nazi policemen, sent to prison, concentration camp, died of typhus.*

We think the author organised the paragraphs like this because **she started with a wide view and narrowed down to focus on Anne. She started with the dangers to** <u>all</u> **Jewish children in Hitler's time, then she talked about those who went into hiding in places like Holland, next she set the scene about Anne and finally the picture story gave the details of Anne's life. It was like in a film where you see the big picture first and then it narrows in to one person.'**

---

## Getting ready

1.  Read the frame out loud and talk about the presentation with your partner.

2.  Read each section of the frame again. Talk about the best way to finish it. Jot down key words to remind you.

3.  Go back and check it through. Have you chosen the best words? Is there anything you need to change or add? (You can add extra sentences if you want.)

4.  Practise your presentation together, taking turns to say one section each. Read the words of the frame, then finish the section in your own words.

5.  Listen to each other and make improvements. Practise till you can do it easily.

**Talking about books**

.......... and I have read.......... .

It was written by .................... and published by

................. .in................(date)

It is set in ...................................... .

The main characters are .................................... .

This is the story in a nutshell............

This is what we liked about the book ................... .

This is what we didn't like about the book............

Here is an extract from the book which gives you a flavour of the author's writing style.................................

(choose a short passage to read out)

## The Furbles of Tarp
*(by Charles Cripps)*

Read the short extract below and answer the questions in complete sentences.

The Pobers quickly became experts in furble craft. They cooded their trish-and-lant furbles, surrounding the tip with a tampit of tarpen dowlies.

- Q. What were the Pobers expert in?

- Q. What did they do with their trish-and-lant furbles?

## Lesson plan: using inferential skills and developing predictive skills

### Based on Dfes Literacy Progress Unit: *Reading Between the Lines*

*Objectives:* To be able to pick out evidence related to setting.

*Big picture:* What differences between the lifestyle of the British and the Americans are apparent to the students? Brainstorm in pairs and later in groups. Consider language, spelling, size of countries, distances, etc.

*Establish the context:* Read excerpt from *The Eighteenth Emergency* by Betsy Byers. In pairs, list the linguistic devices which establish the extract as an American piece.

*Model:* Describe any personal experiences. What Americans would give you if you asked for chips, etc.

*Try:* List all the American words and their English equivalents in pairs and then in a group of four. Share findings with group as a whole. The same procedure will apply to English and American spellings.

*Apply:* 'Use detective skills' to list all the questions to which we do not have answers, e.g. How old is he? What is he running from? Students will effectively create their own writing frame from which to decide the answers. Prompt questions and further writing support in form of writing frames and key vocabulary.

*Secure:* Students now give their opinion about what might happen next in the story. They should try to keep the American *tone* where possible.

Students should next be encouraged to think about *how* they have learned and what they have learned.

## Examples from *Macbeth Teaching Pack*

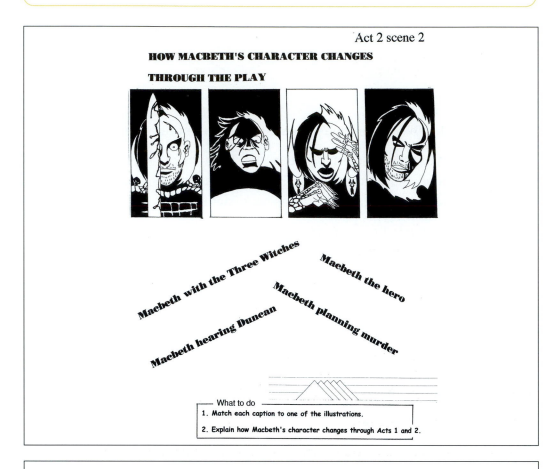

Act 2 scene 2

**HOW MACBETH'S CHARACTER CHANGES**

**THROUGH THE PLAY**

Macbeth with the Three Witches

Macbeth the hero

Macbeth hearing Duncan

Macbeth planning murder

— What to do
1. Match each caption to one of the illustrations.
2. Explain how Macbeth's character changes through Acts 1 and 2.

---

# Act 2 scene 2

**LADY MACBETH'S INSTRUCTIONS**

1. **Get some water**

2. **Wash your hands**

3. **Take the daggers back to Duncan's room
   and wipe the blood off them**

4. **Give me the daggers**

5. **Put on your night gown**

6. **Stop worrying**

**What to do**

1. Read the text pieces   Act 2 scene 2  lines 47-53   55-59   73-75
   What does Lady Macbeth tell Macbeth to do?

2. Find in the text pieces the six instructions Lady Macbeth gives Macbeth.
   Match each instruction to text lines.
   Write down each matching pair.

**Do it like this**

| LADY MACBETH'S INSTRUCTIONS | TEXT LINES |
|---|---|
| Get some water | *Go get some water* <br> *And wash this filthy witness from your hand* <br>            *line 49* |

Cutting Edge Productions

## Key word books and spelling policy

### What could be in a key word booklet for Years 7–9?

- introduction to explain the value and suggested use

- a list of contents

- a section of key words for each English topic

- a list of most commonly used words

- commonly confused words with examples for correct use

- suggestions for proof-reading work

- approaches for remembering spellings

### GCSE booklet

To include all of the above and:

- study techniques, e.g. SQ3R, mind-maps

- methods for revision – day after, week after, etc.

- coursework deadline dates

- writing types, e.g. persuasion, argument, recount, instruction

- exam words, e.g. *analyse, assess, discuss, comment on, compare, contrast, criticise*, etc.

### Structure

<u>Without definition</u>

- Gives opportunity to focus on spelling

- Gives opportunity for dictionary work

- Reinforces knowledge and revision through collecting definitions

- Encourages pupils' responsibility for immediate access to meaning

<u>With definition</u>

- Gives the opportunity to learn spelling and meaning at the same time

- Familiarises pupils with dictionary format

- Builds pupil confidence in dictionary use

- Gives pupils and teachers a resource

## Who wants to be a millionaire?
*Spelling and vocabulary practice*

## Instructions

- Two teams each have a different set of words to test their spelling skills. Each team also has the correct answers to their opponents' word lists.

- One team has a go at selecting the correct word. If they get it right they get four points.

- If they have to go 50–50 and then get it right, they get two points.

- If they get it wrong, the game goes to their opponents.

- They get an additional two points if they show they know what it means by putting the word in a sentence. If they have to 'ask the audience' (a dictionary), they only get one point.

You can probably think of some other ideas! This game can, of course, be specifically related to a chosen topic.

### 'Who wants to be a millionaire?' spelling sheet 1

| 1 | 2 | 3 | 4 |
|---|---|---|---|
| pytee | pity | pitee | pitty |
| mathamatics | mathermatics | mathmatics | mathematics |
| gallop | galop | gallep | galep |
| violence | violance | vialense | vyalense |
| begining | biginning | beginning | begginning |
| separate | seperate | seprate | seperat |
| vallies | vallees | vallys | valleys |
| accessory | acsessory | accesory | accessorie |
| arguement | argument | argumant | arguemant |
| extremeley | extremly | extremly | extremely |
| knoledge | knowledge | knowlidge | nowledge |
| pecculiar | peculiar | peculliar | perculiar |
| volantary | voluntry | volluntary | voluntary |
| outrageouss | outrajeous | outragous | outrageous |
| occassion | ocasion | occasion | occashion |
| desperate | dessperate | desparate | desparatte |
| parallell | parallel | paralel | paralell |
| resistance | resistence | resisstence | risistance |

## 'Who wants to be a millionaire?' spelling sheet 2

| 1 | 2 | 3 | 4 |
|---|---|---|---|
| attendence | atendence | attandance | attenndance |
| werever | wherever | whereever | werevar |
| abundance | abundence | abbundance | abunndance |
| consistent | connsistent | consistant | consestant |
| espeshilly | especilly | especially | espeshally |
| perrsistence | persistance | persisstance | persistence |
| relieving | releiving | releeving | reliefing |
| giudance | guidance | guidence | guydence |
| favrite | favorite | favourite | favouritt |
| rhythom | rhythem | rhythm | rythm |
| dissapearance | dissappearance | disappearance | disapeerance |
| imedietly | immediatly | immediately | imediately |
| omited | ommitted | omitted | ohmitted |
| resevoir | reservoir | resservoir | rezevoir |
| jealousy | jelousy | jealosy | jealousie |
| perculier | peculiar | perculiar | peculia |
| busines | bisness | business | buisness |
| diferrence | diference | difference | diffarance |

(See accompanying CD for amendable lists – make the font size bigger, limit the choices etc. as appropriate for pupils.)

## Simplified instructions for starting *Wordbar*

To start *Wordbar* click **W** at the bottom of the screen. Click on the tab marked *Explorer*. It will always appear furthest to the right.

- Click on the folder to display the contents of the folder.
- Left click on a word/phrase to send it into Word.
- Right click on a word/phrase to hear it being spoken.

To add a word to a grid:

- Left click on a cell while holding down the shift key.
- A small window marked *Cell Text* will appear above the cell.
- Type the word and press *Enter*.
- The word or phrase will appear in the grid.

To change the word in the grid, do exactly the same!

You can sort the words alphabetically by selecting *Sort Words* on grid alphabetically in *Grid Properties*. This will happen the next time the grid is displayed.

You can use the *Tab* key instead of *Enter* to move onto the next cell.

To remove a word from the grid, left-click whilst holding down the *Shift* key. Press the *Delete* key to remove any text and press *Enter*.

### Creating a new Wordbar file

Click on the rectangular button that looks like a calculator at the top left of the menu. Choose *New* from the File menu.

On the left of the window there is a list of all the templates available. Click on a name to see a preview of the template. When you have found a suitable one – click *Create*.

*To change the name of a grid or or the background colour* first move the pointer over the tab at the top of the grid. Left click while holding down the *Shift* key on the keyboard. In the new window, type in the name you wish to give this grid. To alter the background colour of the grid click on *Change*. Choose a colour from the selection available and click *OK*. Click on the set button to accept the changes you made.

### Adding a new grid to a Wordbar file

Click on the rectangular button at the top left of the *Wordbar* window. Choose *Add Grid*. A window will appear.

To insert the grid into your current *Wordbar* file click on the *Add* button.

## Vocabulary building game

*Password* is a great game for vocabulary building, and for working on spelling, synonyms and antonyms. It is a truly inclusive experience for students, and makes a good lesson starter or final plenary activity.

The players sit facing the class with their backs to the board. The teams can be based on gender, eye colour, birth date, where pupils come from, etc. Decide who goes first by a toss of the coin; from then on, it's always losers first.

The teacher writes the word on the board so that the class can see it, but not the contestants. Contestant A's team must then try and pass the word to him by giving him *one word* clues. They cannot mime, nor can they give as a clue a non-existent word. A team member raises a hand if he has a clue, and the player picks him. It is important to keep the game moving, so a player gets only five seconds on each clue. The game then moves to the other side.

A clue for 'grass', for example, might be 'green' or 'lawn'. It cannot be 'You cut it with a lawn-mower' or 'Cows eat it' because each of these clues is more than one word. Nor could the clue-giver mime cutting a lawn. If either of these rules is broken, then the turn passes to the other team without a guess. If the clue-giver gives the answer by mistake, then his team loses the point.

Related words can be given as clues, but not plurals, e.g. 'grasses' is not acceptable, but 'grassing' or 'grassed' are. You can also give as a clue words which sound like 'grass', e.g. 'ass' or 'lass'. However, you are not allowed to indicate that the word is a rhyme.

If the player gets the correct word, but gives it in plural form, then the game should be awarded to them.

Occasionally, teams may run out of clues for a given word. If this occurs:

- the teacher can give three quick clues as a tiebreaker; or

- the turn can be declared a stalemate and a new word given.

When a word with one sound but two different meaning and/or spellings is given, e.g. 'dye', the player only has to give the correct word in sound.

One interesting variation of *Password* is to use it as a reinforcer of new learning. I recently had to teach a group with SEN about Islam, and used this game to reinforce new vocabulary.

The word lists are given only as a starter. Teachers know their own students best, and can develop their own lists. (See accompanying CD for amendable copy.)

## Password vocabulary

### Basic

man  run  gun  sun  bed  sad  pin  pet  bag  dog  fog  pig  pen  book
cook  egg  ball  king  sing  song  foot  wood  old  ring  spring  gold
drum  tree  box  sky  milk  cake  game  car  sand  nest  skip  bite
road  ice  drop  cup  paper  jewel  scarf  skeleton  art  ill  onion  pain
black  yellow  star  sunny  jacket  coat  pop  brain  laugh  smile

### Intermediate

lid  bell  sum  boxing  cream  skip  sponge  diamond  fever  roar  can
get  met  feed  hide  bud  fell  win  shop  hill  will  rag  rub  yes  no
bit  bath  look  kill  cap  tap  then  here  hold  bring  wash  want  them
she  who  fix  sweet  name  dish  rich  side  best  rest  today  together
yesterday  play  help  saw  time  keep  never  pilot  nervous  telescope
microscope  athlete  hero  salute  poison  student  university

### Advanced

writer  orphan  permission  juicy  sentence  peace  instant  microwave
fierce  priest  scent  moisture  palm  lungs  parcel  crooked  zone
cinema  debt  doubt  injury  ghost  grudge  chuckle  instrument  ceiling
pistol  jealousy  energy  genuine  respect  design  spell  dream
nightmare  disease  inoculation  innocent  guilty  shade  shadow  you

## Original writing: 'The Assassin' plot, character and setting

This is a writing frame adapted from the Teachit website. It is intended for students with very low confidence in forming their ideas.

'The Assassin' involves a character who is a professional killer. He could be cold blooded, hardened and experienced – or it could be his/her first job. Write a paragraph to describe his/her appearance . Write five sentences.

Describe the *eyes, mouth* and *build* of the assassin. Use some words from the *Wordbar* grid descriptions.

(Having some mugshots handy at this point would obviously suit the more visual learner– and they can readily be found in Clipart. There are other Clipart sites which may be found in the www.ictadvice.co.uk website.)

### Paragraph 1: The killer's wait – setting the scene

- *Do not write anything which suggests why he is there until the final sentence.* Keep your audience guessing.

- Where is s/he? Trees? Long grass? Tower block? Multi-storey car-park?

- Lying down? Standing? Crouching?

- What is the weather like? Rainy? Misty? Sunny? Night time?

- Put your description of your assassin in here. What sort of clothes is he dressed in? Describe them from head to toe. What colours are the clothes? Are they camouflaged?

- Is he cold or too warm? Is he sweating or shivering/shaking? Why?

- What sort of things does he see happening while he waits? Ordinary things, like cars passing down the lonely roads? People walking with dogs and prams? Children playing? Is he worried about hitting them? What does he say to himself?

- Is he cold-blooded and couldn't care less? Or is he on his first job and nervous? Now you deal with her/his guns and weaponry. What are they? How does he make sure that they work? Describe his practice routine.

### Paragraph 2

- Describe the place the assassin is hiding in. Neat? Tidy? Rubbish thrown around? Describe some of the rubbishy bits and some of the dull colours of things that you see – browns, greys, black.

- Describe the weather. Cold? Cloudy? Drizzly rain? Pools of water?

- What might s/he be thinking about? His home? Friends? His last case? [Where was he?] The effect of the bullet on his victim?

## Paragraph 3

- Use this paragraph to describe the arrival of the victim by car. Start the paragraph with a sentence such as 'He turned as an expensive car turned off the road.'

- Is the assassin cool and unhurried or is he shaking and nervous? How do you know?

- How does he prepare his gun?

- Describe some small details to set the scene: mud streaks on the car, a damaged bumper. A bystander blocking his view.

## Paragraph 4

- In this paragraph deal with the victim and the killing.

- Is the victim a man or a woman? Old or young? Important? Well-dressed? Shabby?

- How would s/he move from car to house? Slowly? Carefree? Nervous?

- There might be muddy puddles. What might be reflected in them?

- Delay the killing until the end of the paragraph. How does the assassin line up his victim in his sights? Describe the echoes of the shot and the effect of the hit.

## Paragraph 5

- The assassin moves away from the scene. (Slowly? Calmly? Jerkily?)

- He needs to pack away his rifle, carefully check he hasn't left anything (cigarette ends, cartridge case) and move away towards his car.

- Is he still calm? Is he pouring with sweat? Breathing heavily? Shaking? Or just cool (unruffled?) Does he phone anyone? Does he use a mobile? What does he say?

The *Wordbar* grid would appear at the bottom of the computer screen but would not look like this! You should look at the Crick website to get the idea. You could download other grids or design them yourself to accompany other paragraphs here.

| bloodshot | close-set | cold | piercing | cruel |
|-----------|-----------|--------|-----------|----------|
| solid? | heavy? | stocky? | chunky? | thin? |
| cruel | frowning | thin | grinning | drooping |
| | | | | |

## Written response to *Macbeth* by William Shakespeare

- READ the questions below carefully.

- LOOK up the page references given and SEARCH for relevant information. (Page references given are for *Macbeth: The Shorter Shakespeare* published by Carel Press.)

- MAKE NOTES in the spaces after each question.

- Use your notes to WRITE A FULL ANSWER to each question on file paper. The beginning of each answer is started for you.

- You might like to use your notes to write an essay entitled 'Explore the characters of Macbeth and Lady Macbeth in the play'. Use the opening lines given to begin each new PARAGRAPH.

---

1) *What do we learn about Macbeth at the beginning of the play?*
   (LOOK at p. 6, the second half of p. 12 and p. 17.)

   At the beginning of the play Macbeth is ...

2) *How does Lady Macbeth support Macbeth in his ambition to become king?*
   (LOOK at Act 1, scene 5, p. 14 and p. 16.)

   Lady Macbeth feels that Macbeth is 'too full o' th' milk of human kindness' to murder King Duncan. She tries to support him by ...

3) *Why does Macbeth begin to change his mind about murdering King Duncan in Act 1, scene 7?* (LOOK at his speech on p. 18 from the line 'He's here in double trust ...')

Macbeth is reluctant to murder Duncan because ...

4) *How does Lady Macbeth react when Macbeth decides* not *to commit the murder?* What does she say to Macbeth? (LOOK at the second half of p. 18, p. 19 and p. 20.)

When Lady Macbeth learns that her husband has changed his mind she is ... She tells him ...

5) *When Macbeth and his wife become king and queen of Scotland, they do not enjoy their new positions. Explain why this is.* (LOOK particularly at Macbeth's speech on p. 37 in Act 3, scene 1.)

Macbeth and Lady Macbeth do not enjoy being king and queen because ...

6) *How does Macbeth behave when he faces Macduff in Act 5, scene 6?* (LOOK at p. 70 and particularly the top of p. 71) THINK ABOUT the following questions to help you answer this: is Macbeth sorry that he killed Macduff's family?

How does he face defeat?

Is he brave or cowardly at the end?

In Act 5, scene 1, Macbeth seems ...

7) *In your opinion, is Macbeth or Lady Macbeth the more guilty in the play?* Try to give at least two reasons for your answer.

I think that ⎯⎯⎯⎯ is the more guilty because ...

## How to paint a bathroom wall

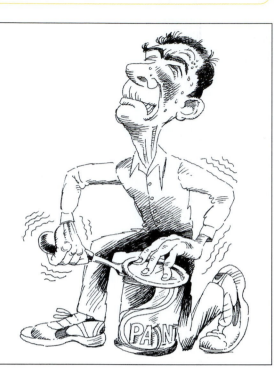

- Get a paint brush.

- Get two tins of paint: an undercoat and a top coat.

- Open the first tin.

- Put the paint brush in the paint pot.

- Paint the wall all over.

- Let it dry.

- Clean your brush.

- Open the second tin.

- Cover the first coat with a second coat.

## Activity

As a group or in pairs, pupils can consider the inadequacies of the instructions as they stand (i.e. lack of detail). If the instructions are left in the middle of a large sheet of paper they can make annotations around them.

The *How? What? Where? When? Why?* questions should stimulate some answers.

The wordbar below can be used to support pupils' own versions of the instructions.

| At first/ To start | To start with | First | At the beginning | Then |
|---|---|---|---|---|
| After that | Next | Finally | Another thing | Be careful to |
| I discovered | I learnt | I found out | I thought | I saw |
| Do not let... | Check that it... | Check for the... | Follow the... | I discovered... |

## Lesson plan: fact and opinion

*Objectives*: To recognise the difference between facts and opinions, and also to be aware that sometimes it can be difficult to distinguish between the two.

*Establish the context*: Read two witness statements to an accident which has involved a boy who gets knocked down by a car. Explain that they may well be involved in such a situation in the future and it is important to be sure of the facts.

*Big picture*: Ask for any personal experiences of accident situations – we have to be careful here! This will consolidate their understanding as only the facts will be requested.

*Model*: Describe any personal experiences. Give students a cloze exercise of a witness statement with key phrases missing. Ask them to complete it.

Ask for their *opinion* about the most dangerous driving situations (think about weather conditions, type of driver, age, experience).

*Try*: Consider the witness statements (below) and decide whether what they write is fact or opinion. Take each sentence and record your views beside it. Discuss with partner where you agree and disagree.

*Apply*: Write the accident statement of the victim (the boy) keeping to the facts. Give prompt questions and further writing support in form of writing frames and key vocabulary.

*Secure*: Students now give their opinion about who they think is mainly to blame and also to voice their opinion on how such accidents could be avoided in the future. Present their findings in the form of a poster about accident prevention.

Students will now be encouraged to think about *how* they have learned and what they have learned.

## Witness statements

I was waiting for my father to pick me up outside the school gates at twenty past eleven on the night of 27 April. I had been to see 'Macbeth' at the Royal Shakespeare Theatre with most of Year 11 from the school.

The coach had arrived back at school about ten minutes before, and had driven up the drive and dropped us at the main school entrance. Most of the pupils had gone straight back down the drive to where their parents were waiting in their cars, near the school gates. A lot of people had driven off fairly quickly, but my father was late. A few pupils had not yet come down the drive. My father was going to give Andrew McIntyre and Mark Bishop a lift home as they both live near us.

Andrew and Mark were kicking an empty can around by the gates because they were tired of waiting. Andrew knocked it into the road accidentally, and Mark stepped off the pavement to kick it back, but just at that moment, a motor cyclist came over the brow of the hill, going much faster than the speed limit. Fortunately, Mark was able to leap sideways, and so the motorcycle only knocked him into the side of a parked car. If Mark had not been so quick, he would have been killed. The motorcyclist obviously did not think that anyone would be around the school at that time of night.

Witness A

I was parked outside the school gates at twenty past eleven on 27 April. The coach had got back from Stratford at about eleven ten, and had parked in the school grounds somewhere. My son had not yet appeared, although a lot of the Year 11 pupils had already come out of the school grounds, and been driven off by their parents.

Two of the pupils still waiting by the gates were messing around and making a lot of noise. I thought that they had probably been drinking on the coach because they were so rowdy and they were kicking an empty cider can around.

One boy deliberately kicked it into the road, and the other dashed out between two parked cars to get it. The motorcyclist could not possibly have known the boy was going to dart out from between the cars. He braked hard and so, fortunately, only struck the boy a glancing blow.

Witness B

## Writing frame for a critical evaluation of a poem

.................................................. and I have been discussing

.................................................. by ..................................................... .

This is a classic/modern poem about ...............................................................

............................................................................................................... .

The main theme/message of the poem is ........................................................

............................................................................................................... .

We found this (un)interesting because ..........................................................

............................................................................................................... .

The style of the poem is illustrated in this extract:

............................................................................................................... .

We think this is (in)effective because ..........................................................

............................................................................................................... .

The poet uses imagery/word play such as ....................................................

............................................................................................................... .

In our opinion, this is (un)successful because .............................................

............................................................................................................... .

We think the best/worst line in the poem is

............................................................................................................... .

We (dis)like it because ...............................................................................  .

On the whole, this poem makes us feel .........................................................

because ................................................................................................... .

## Worked example

Chris and I have been discussing *The Charge of the Light Brigade* by Alfred, Lord Tennyson. This is a classic poem about a brigade of soldiers in the Crimean War, who were given the wrong orders. They were told to charge directly at the enemy's guns. When they obeyed the order, most of the soldiers died. Tennyson was Poet Laureate at the time and he wrote this poem to commemorate them.

The main message of the poem is that the Charge of the Light Brigade was glorious because the soldiers put duty before their own lives. We found this interesting because nowadays the excuse that 'I was only following orders' is not considered a very good one, and the newspapers tell us that suicide bombers are evil.

The style of the poem is illustrated in this extract:

'"Forward, the Light Brigade"/Was there a man dismayed?/Not though the soldiers knew/Someone had blundered./Theirs not to make reply,/Theirs not to reason why,/Theirs but to do and die:/Into the Valley of Death/Rode the six hundred.'

We think this is effective because the rhyme and repetition carry you along like the soldiers' horses. The repetition of 'Theirs' hammers home the importance of duty. The last two lines have a slower rhythm that makes them seem more solemn

The poet uses imagery such as 'jaws of Death, mouth of Hell'. In our opinion, this is successful because the images conjured up are simple but terrifying.

We think the best lines in the poem are 'Stormed at with shot and shell,/While horse and hero fell,/They that had fought so well/Came through the jaws of Death,/Back from the mouth of Hell,/All that was left of them,/Left of six hundred.' We like them because they repeat lots of lines we've heard before, but this time they're coming back and we realise most of the soldiers are dead. Tennyson doesn't say how many were left, but we've found out it was about 200 – so two out of three died.

On the whole, the poem makes us feel sad but proud because although it was a mistake, Tennyson makes you see the glory of what they did. It also makes you understand how other nations might feel differently from us about their suicide bombers.

### *Jabberwocky* writing frame

*Fit a noun or an adjective in the gaps and make your own poem.*

'Twas _____ *adj*, and the _____ *adj* _____ *n*
Did gyre and gimble in the _____ *n*;
All                    *adj* were the                    *n*;
And the _____ *adj* _____ *n* outgrabe.

'Beware the Jabberwock, my son!
The jaws that bite, the claws that catch!
Beware the Jubjub bird, and shun (avoid)
The _____ *adj* Bandersnatch!'

He took his _____ *adj* sword in hand:
Long time the _____ *adj* foe (enemy) he sought (looked for) –
So rested he by the Tumtum tree,
And stood awhile in thought.

And, as in _____ *adj* thought he stood,
The Jabberwock, with eyes of flame,
Came whiffling through the _____ *adj* wood,
And burbled as it came!

One two! One two! And through and through
The _____ *adj* blade went snicker-snack!
He left it dead, and with its head
He went galumphing back.

'And hast thou (have you) slain (killed) the Jabberwock?
Come to my arms, my _____ *adj* boy!
O _____ *adj* day! Callooh! Callay!'
He chortled (laughed) in his joy.

'Twas _____ *adj*, and the _____ *adj* _____ *n*
Did gyre and gimble in the _____ *n*:
All _____ *adj* were the _____ *n*,
And the _____ *adj* _____ *n* outgrabe.

Lewis Carroll

## Word bank for *Jabberwocky*

| NOUN – the name we give to something, e.g. car, table or monster. | ADJECTIVE – a word that describes (gives us more information about) a noun, e.g. the terrifying monster. |
|---|---|
| farms | gentle |
| rocks | peaceful |
| mountains | deadly |
| waterfall | terrifying |
| ruins | foolish |
| waves | deep |
| clouds | quiet |
| dragons | wonderful |
| swamps | dark |
| toads | ghostly |
| creepers | brave |
| snakes | cheerful |
| fish | freezing |
| spirits | slimy |
| lizards | friendly |
| rats | sultry |
| badgers | vast |
| pigs | chilly |
| mudflats | warm |
| sea | oppressive |
| wood | leathery |
| sky | bad-tempered |
| fields | creepy |
| undergrowth | tiny |
| cave | icy |
| jungle | sharp |
| orchards | misty |
| | twisted |
| | furious |
| | humorous |
| | angry |
| | joyful |
| | threatening |
| | miserable |
| | excited |
| | gloomy |
| | fierce |
| | laughing |
| | victorious |

## Homework ideas

When planning homework tasks, remember to take into account the amount of time some pupils will need to spend and differentiate accordingly. Compile a list of activities which do not involve any writing:

- List three things that you have learnt today. (Confirm in the plenary what those three things might be and supply key vocabulary to support them.)

- Create a poster to illustrate the spelling strategy you have learnt. Use colour, mnemonics and pictures, e.g. Think of the para (chutist) in se*para*te, the *pie*ce of pie.

- Write down ten questions you would like to ask a character in the book we are currently studying.

- Take some key descriptive vocabulary and make up an incorrect spelling for one word to go with the correct spelling and test it out on classmates in the next lesson.

- Using supplied adjectives, design an advertisement for a book or film that is being studied. Take pictures from Clipart if you have a computer. Use pictures from magazines if you haven't got access to a computer.

- Use the worksheet facility of *ClozePro* to generate a cloze exercise based on the theme under discussion.

- Cut out five photographs from today's newspaper. See if you can make up new captions for them. Write the first two sentences of the story that accompanies them (from your imagination).

- Watch a holiday programme on TV and state which of the destinations you liked best and why. An extension of this could be to include a description of the one you most disliked and why.

- Listen to a short story on tape (borrow a tape recorder if necessary). Give it a mark out of ten according to various criteria (attention holding, believable characters, humour, shock value, sadness, etc.)

- Write a menu for one meal that you have had today. Using supplied vocabulary, try and make it sound as exciting as possible. Use Word or Publisher if you want.

- Persuade your teacher that the sports team you support or the club you belong to is the best in the world (use supplied vocabulary/writing frame).

## Pupil self-evaluation sheet

### How good a writer am I?

|  | Always | Sometimes | Never |
|---|---|---|---|
| **When I write:** | | | |
| I make a rough plan before I start | ☐ | ☐ | ☐ |
| I find out any information I need to know | ☐ | ☐ | ☐ |
| **I check my writing by asking myself:** | | | |
| Have I missed anything out? | ☐ | ☐ | ☐ |
| Is it in the right order? | ☐ | ☐ | ☐ |
| Does it say what I want it to say? | ☐ | ☐ | ☐ |
| Could I use better words? | ☐ | ☐ | ☐ |
| Is it interesting? | ☐ | ☐ | ☐ |
| Have I got a good title? | ☐ | ☐ | ☐ |
| Before re-drafting, I check my writing for spelling and punctuation. | ☐ | ☐ | ☐ |

I am good at: ............................................................................................

Not so good at: ........................................................................................

Spelling    Writing in sentences    Using capital letters    Handwriting    Using commas
Using speech marks    Writing in paragraphs    Using interesting words

This is what I need to do to improve:   take more time to plan                ☐

practise my handwriting         ☐

check my punctuation            ☐

take more care with spellings   ☐

get someone to read my work
and give me some useful
feedback                        ☐

# Individual Education Plans

## King Edward VI School, Bury St Edmunds   INDIVIDUAL EDUCATION PLAN (IEP)   School Action/Action Plus

| Name: Shannon Craig | Date of Birth: | Yr group: 9 | Form: | IEP Start Date: | Review Date: |
|---|---|---|---|---|---|

**Pen Portrait:** Shannon has worked hard to overcome her difficulties but still has significant problems with reading and spelling – and it may be that she has lost confidence since joining Upper school.

**Areas to be developed:** Continuing to work on her reading and spelling and developing her confidence in speaking. Helping her to organise and extend her thoughts in preparation for speaking.

| Targets | Strategies | Provision | Success Criteria | Achieved |
|---|---|---|---|---|
| 1. To ask relevant questions during a class lesson | • Use cue cards with words such as 'because' and 'why?' to help her develop her answers to questions. | • Set of cards with prepared questions, worked through with Shannon. | • Asks appropriate questions at the end of a lesson. <br>• Selects appropriate cue cards before the lesson. | |
| 2. To raise reading level by at least one year by November | • Check that Shannon has read and understood multi-syllable words. <br>• Read out complex/new words to class to check understanding. | • Home-school reading agreement – 5 sessions/week for 10–15 minutes. <br>• Shannon 's choice of fiction – some from magazines with supported paired reading. | • Reading level improved and verified by testing – April. | |
| 3. To identify words and phrases not understood | • When she finds terms that she doesn't know Shannon will highlight them for clarification in her exercise books <br>• Construct a personal word bank and definitions (ICT). | • Use of Word on computer 3 sessions a week in the mornings and/or lunchtimes. | • Shannon is able to develop a greater sense of understanding. <br>• Shannon takes more responsibility for identifying areas of difficulty. | |

**Parent/Carer Involvement:** Access to computer at home. Reinforce subject-specific words. Participate in reading programme – follow published guidance.

**Pupil's View:** Shannon feels reasonably OK about targets with the exception of the first – after discussion was prepared to give it a try (subject to early review in February).

**Additional Information:** Shannon has benefited from the use of coloured overlays which have reduced 'paper glare' but is rather self-conscious about using them.

**Evaluation and future action:**

Names of all staff involved

Signed: _____   (SENCO) Date: _____

**Continued**

## King Edward VI School, Bury St Edmunds   INDIVIDUAL EDUCATION PLAN (IEP)   School Action/Action Plus

| Name: *Dinesh Kumar* | Date of Birth: | Yr group: 9 | Form: | IEP Start Date: | Review Date: |
|---|---|---|---|---|---|

**Pen Portrait:** Dinesh has made progress with his reading and in small groups has shown more confidence in speaking. Listening skills need to be nurtured – he can misunderstand the task set and needs careful monitoring in this regard.

**Areas to be developed:** Spelling, organisation and presentational skills all need to be developed. Dinesh can become easily confused by multi-part instructions.

| Targets | Strategies | Provision | Success Criteria | Achieved |
|---|---|---|---|---|
| 1. To produce pieces of independent writing using Word | ● Use Word in conjunction with *Wordbar* to provide support with spelling and structuring writing. | ● Use computer in base for independent writing – all subjects.<br>● Use PC at home for homework.<br>● Support from TA. | ● Three pieces of writing produced independently. | |
| 2. To use the spelling tool on a computer to check and correct spellings | ● Encourage Dinesh to use computerised word bank when working independently. | ● Computer's own spell check facility and spelling tool.<br>● Use of published guidance.<br>● Assemble own word bank. | ● Observed to use spelling tool independently in the course of 3 pieces of work. | |
| 3. To produce more readable handwriting | ● Use of peer support to identify neat letter formation. Unjoining 'tailed' letters.<br>● Peer to provide reminders in lesson time. | ● Experimentation to find most suitable pen.<br>● TA to check that all basic equipment present (ruler, pencil etc.) | ● Handwriting /presentation skills improve by Easter.<br>● Peer and TA both agree with Dinesh's judgement! | |

**Parent/Carer Involvement:**
To support Dinesh in improving presentation skills and to monitor use of computer at home. Check spelling on his personal word bank.

**Pupil's View:**
Dinesh completely agrees with the above targets but worries about his ability to improve his handwriting.

**Additional Information:**
Check that Dinesh understands the nature of the task set with the question: 'What do you have to do?'

**Evaluation and future action:**

Names of all staff involved

Signed: _____ (SENCO) Date: _____

## Learning support systems – a description

In order to obtain 'value for money' both for staff and students, it is desirable that an agreement is drawn up between subject staff and support staff. This will ensure that both parties know what is required and expected. The contract may identify specific children in need of support and the ways they are to be supported.

It should be recognised that it may not always be appropriate for Learning Support staff to be in a lesson for part, or even all of the time if, for instance, the teacher is to read to a class.

### Sixth form students

Older students who have *volunteered* to support in the classroom are there as an extra pair of hands. They are there as people to whom anyone in the class, rather than specified individuals, can turn for assistance.

#### Help can include:

- preparation of learning materials (e.g. paper, books, videos)

- reading and explaining tasks

- helping in discussion work

- helping students to organise their work

- acting as a student–teacher link

- hearing students read.

### Teaching Assistant

TA's timetable may be linked to an individual or a group of students.

#### Help can include:

- working primarily with pupils on School Action and School Action +, but nevertheless to be regarded as a whole-class resource

- targeting individual pupils in order to support numeracy skills

- assisting students with reading/explaining subject texts/worksheets/taking notes from whiteboards or from yourself

- assisting with the reviews of targets within a pupil's IEP

- scribing for pupils with specific needs, e.g. pupils with physical impairment/specific writing difficulties

- acting as a student–teacher link where the student cannot communicate effectively

- helping in discussion work

- supporting higher-order reading skills/retrieval of information

- supporting and encouraging pupils with low self-esteem/lack of self-confidence and poor motivation

- extracting a small group (maximum five) to work on specific tasks under your direction. This should not be a group comprised solely of children with behavioural difficulties

- supporting pupils with organisational difficulties

- assistance with physical and practical tasks

- supporting pupils with behavioural and emotional difficulties

- being an extra adult when students go out of school

- modify your worksheets/texts, exam and test papers to enable greater access for all students in your group, under guidance from the SENCO

- keep an accurate log/diary of their activities within the classroom situation, noting a student's progress and/or difficulties.

### A Teaching Assistant should not be expected to:

- be left alone with a class (see below)

- mark work, other than the occasional correction (e.g. spelling) at the student's side and with your agreement.

## Senior (Advanced) Teaching Assistant

This is a supervisory level post which involves the supervision of other TAs and of classes in the absence of the teacher.

### Help can include:

- organising and monitoring the work of other TAs including timetabling, rosters and absence cover as appropriate

- teaching small groups to enhance their literacy and numeracy skills

- maintaining and collating records of pupil needs and progress

- organising and scheduling annual review meetings/review meetings of students on SA and SA+

- organising the special examination circumstances of students with special educational needs. This may involve liaison with middle schools, examination officers, exam boards, subject heads and parents. It also involves organising appropriate venues

- attending and contributing to SEN and other review meetings if required by the head teacher and, where appropriate, disseminate information to other TAs

- supervising classes (up to five a week) in the absence of their teacher, chiefly in the 'Faculty of expertise'.

## Learning Support Teacher

These are trained teachers with classroom experience and further professional qualifications in the field of special needs. They are most effectively used within a 'team-teaching' role.

You may expect them to contribute directly to the teaching of the group and they may, in effect, operate a dialogue with you and with the students. They will help set and mark work, and may cover for you when you are absent.

### *Help can include:*

- supporting pupils with behavioural and emotional difficulties

- supporting and encouraging pupils with low self-esteem/lack of self-confidence and poor motivation

- assessing monitor and review pupils on the SEN register

- targeting individual pupils in order to support numeracy skills

- advising on preparing teaching materials in collaboration with you and/or with your department/faculty

- advising on modifying your worksheets/texts, exam and test papers to enable greater access for all students in your group

- obtaining outside advice regarding exam concessions

- advising on exercises in differentiation

- carrying out additional assessments as requested and as deemed necessary

- seeking out appropriate material and/or equipment for special needs of all kinds from outside resources. Work out and operate behaviour strategies with you

- giving information/advice on specific learning problems

- observing, feeding back and planning services for individuals and groups.

# Resources and contact details

## Addresses

Crick Software Ltd: Crick House, Boarden Close, Moulton Park, Northampton NN3 6LF Tel: 0845 121 1691 Fax: 0845 121 1692

Cutting Edge Publications: Pill Farmhouse, Lostwithiel, Cornwall PL22 0JR Tel: 01208 872337

ianSYST Ltd: The White House, 72 Fen Road, Cambridge CB4 1UN Tel: 01223 420101 (Source of electronic hardware)

NFER-Nelson: Darville House, 2 Oxford Road East, Windsor, Berks SL4 1DF Tel: 01753 858961

## Websites

www.becta.org.uk: British educational and communications technology association
www.calsc.co.uk: Jane Mitchell's site. Dedicated to learning memory training
www.crossboweducation.co.uk: Lots of word games and Irlen materials
www.eriding.net/amoore/default.htm: Andrew Moore's website. Excellent resources
http://www.donjohnston.com: for Co:Writer
www.smartpass.co.uk: Tel: 01483 237275
www.tagdev.co.uk: or www.taglearning.com: Source of electronic learning hardware
www.teachit.co.uk: Source of excellent resources
www.texthelp.com: Tel: 028 94 428105 Fax: 02894428574

Becta also recommends the following site for 'powerful but cheap computers': http://www.everythingeducation.org

Some other sites that sell second-hand and cheap PCs include:

www.computerbargains.co.uk
www.indigopc.com
www.morgancomputers.co.uk
www.sterlingxs.co.uk
www.tekexpress.co.uk

# References

Buckroyd, P. (2003) *AQA English GCSE Specification A: Revising AQA English.* Oxford: OUP.

Crewe, J. (2003) *AQA English Specification A – AQA A Support Book.* Oxford: OUP.

Dethridge, T. and Dethridge, M. (2002) *Literacy Through Symbols.* London: David Fulton Publishers.

DfEE (2001) *Literacy Progress Unit: Reading Between the Lines.* London: HMSO.

DfES (2004) *Removing Barriers to Achievement: The Government's Strategy for SEN,* London: HMSO.

Gross, J. (2003) 'Time for a Change' *Special,* Autumn, 12–14.

*Headwork* English programme series, OUP.

McKeown, S. (2000) *Unlocking Potential: How ICT Can Support Children With Special Needs.* Birmingham: Questions Publishing Co. Ltd.

Ofsted (2003) *Good Assessment Practice in English.* London: HMSO.

Palmer, S. (2004) *Speaking Frames.* London: David Fulton Publishers.

Powell, R. (1997) *Active Whole-class Teaching.* Stafford: Robert Powell Publications.

Rustin, L. *et al.* (2001) *Stammering: A practical guide for teachers and other professionals.* London: David Fulton Publishers.

Smith, A. *Accelerated Learning in the Classroom.* Stafford: Network Educational Press Ltd.

Smith, D. *Specific Learning Difficulties.* NASEN.

Squires, G. and McKeown, S. (2003) *Supporting Children with Dyslexia.* Birmingham: Questions Publishing Company.

Stakes, R. and Hornby, G. (2000) *Meeting Special Needs in Mainstream Schools: A Practical Guide for Teachers.* London: David Fulton Publishers.

*The Inclusive Readers Series.* London: David Fulton Publishers.

Turner, E. and Pughe, J. (2003) *English and Dyslexia.* London: David Fulton Publishers.

Waines, J. *AQA: A Support Teacher's Book.* Oxford: OUP.

Walker, D. (2002) 'Resources for Action Research'. Unpublished.